Freddy's Magic Garden

Incredible Cat Stories by Kitty Freddy and His Friends

Angelina Dayan

with
Helen Nicholson & Andy Shepheard

Angelina Dayan Publishing

ISBN 9798842429806

ASIN B0B7GRTVHW

Freddy's Magic Garden

You inspired this book, my sweet kitties,

It is to you that I owe it,

It is to you that I dedicate it.

THANKS

Thank you, my Twitter friends, my first readers, of whom I only know the first name or the name of your kitty! Your cheering words have given me the confidence to continue writing and publishing these stories. Thank you, Maureen, Andy, Helen, Ulrike, Ruth, Sherri, Debra, Sue, Cilla, and so many others.

Many thanks to Emmy, my editor, for her dedication (and to Isobella for wagging her tail in approval).

Special thanks to my brilliant guest writers, Andy Shepheard (Maggie) and Helen Nicholson (Munch), for their kind participation. Freddy and I are so happy to have you with us!

Contents

Preface

One night, during a terrible storm, I picked up a little black and white kitten from the pavement and took it home. I had no idea of the space that this little being – freezing, starving and soaked to the bone – would occupy in my life. For you see, the moment his tiny paws crossed the threshold of the front door, he ceased to be a cat. He became Freddy, the most beloved little kitty-boy to me and my seven Maine Coon cats. His arrival turned our house into an enchanted place and our garden into a magic garden. The sun he brought with him brightened our days even when it rained.

Like a happy little fur ball, he starts each day with crazy games, runs around the house, plays catch-me-if-you-can with an imaginary pursuer and hides behind doors, calling us to come and find him. And when we comply, he jumps on us and dashes away to another hiding place. When he gets tired, he comes in to settle down and shower everyone with his little kisses and cuddles before running out into the garden for more adventures.

That said, you may be wondering why Freddy is the author of this book – and not I, his Mum.

I always wanted to have just one cat, but as you will discover in the pages of this book, one thing led to another, and I ended up with 15 kitties – sometimes more – either in the house or as permanent garden guests.

Many of them have experienced incredible adversity. Fortunately, all their ordeals have had happy endings. My gang of cats are almost all special and have provided the material for the stories in this book. We have been through much fear and anxiety together, but also shared many moments of relief and joy.

However, it was only when I started to tell some of their adventures on social media networks and saw the enthusiasm of my friends who wanted to know more, who waited impatiently for each new story, that I decided to gather them into a book.

That way, you, too, my reader, can enjoy them.

But then I encountered a problem. As I sat in front of my screen and started to line up one word after another, the results were never as good as I wanted them to be. Then one day, just as I was about to give up, Freddy came to my rescue. He jumped on my desk and exclaimed: "Meow, Mum, I'll show you how to do it! You don't know how to tell stories. I'll tell you what to say. You just need to do the typing"

At least, that's what I seemed to hear. So I allowed him to continue "speaking" and used his voice to channel the stories. It was a relief to have this free-spirited little boy's influence, and everything flowed from there. I think sometimes he added a little too much of his cat craziness, and sometimes his imagination may have strayed a little too far. It's up to you to decide, dear reader, whether he has done a good job.

However, we both hope these stories will bring you a few happy moments.

Let the stories begin!

Mum (Angelina Dayan), the co-author

Chapter One

IN WHICH KITTY FREDDY AND HIS LITTLE
FAMILY ALMOST STARVE TO DEATH AND GO
THROUGH MANY ROLLER-COASTER
ADVENTURES.

The Vacant Lot

We came into the world in the springtime on a vacant lot, my sister Caramel and I. Our Mummy cat (Maman, we used to call her) was a little black kitty and practically still a kitten herself. We were her first litter. The weather was scorching that spring, and Maman, who had no experience being a mummy, soon ran into a desperate situation. Only two weeks after our birth, all three of us almost died of hunger and thirst.

Luckily, a miracle happened. Here is the whole story.

Expecting What?

Once upon a time, a little black kitty lived on a vacant lot not far from a large park. When the weather was nice and warm, she stayed home. A giant chestnut tree stood in the corner farthest from the street, and it was nice to sleep on the dry leaves that had accumulated under it over the years.

The kitty sought refuge elsewhere when it rained or the weather was chilly. Sometimes she would sneak through a broken window into Mrs. Martin's cellar in the neighbouring house. Another option was Peter's sheltered terrace, a few houses away. The old man kept a large paper coal sack, convenient for frosty nights. The kitty would slip into the bottom of the bag, make herself a nest, roll up in a ball and fall asleep. Of course, she would emerge all covered in soot in the morning, but it didn't matter: her fur was black anyway! She just had to shake it up a little bit.

This was her life, the same as her mother's had been before her and her granny's. Whole generations of black cats had lived on that vacant lot, one after another. Nobody knew why there weren't several cats at a time or where the previous renter of the lot had gone. Naturally, finding food was a daily problem. To eat, the little black kitty would go through garbage or pilfer food from gardens. There were plenty of dogs in the neighbourhood, and their bowls were usually well-stocked. But she had to be careful not to get caught by one of them.

Then one day, as her first birthday approached, she felt something change in her body. Her belly was becoming rounder and heavier, and something was even starting to move in there! What could it be? It was frightening, wasn't it?

That night she complained to her friend, Rosalie, an old ginger cat from the park. The old lady was said to be her grand-grand-grand auntie. Cat generations follow each other very quickly, it seems.

"You're expecting, my dear!" exclaimed Rosalie. She had been through this many times when she was younger.

"Expecting what?" The black kitty couldn't remember ordering anything, so what should she expect?

"Babies, my dear, babies! Little kittens are in there! Get ready, start looking for a house!"

The black kitty was at a loss. The area where she lived was very posh, and the square footage was among the most expensive in the whole country. She had checked the property advertisements, sniffing the hedges in the gardens here and there. But oh dear, all the beautiful houses were already taken: the cave inside the woodshed, which would have been so convenient; the one-room apartment inside the rhododendron bush; and this beautiful home on soft, dry leaves in Mrs Martin's hedge! All were occupied, and none of the owners was willing to swap for a coal bag or a damp cellar. It seemed impossible to find a family home in the neighbourhood unless you were a millionaire. And she wasn't – her only fortune was a champagne cork and a small piece of red ribbon, which she cherished too much to exchange.

She turned to Rosalie. "Auntie Rosalie, can you help me?"

"Well, my dear, look around you! Sometimes the obvious escapes us," said Rosalie and trotted away. She was not concerned about housing: she had the whole park to herself. Ah, wealthy relatives are so selfish at times!

But what did she mean by "the obvious"? Black kitty looked around and couldn't see any suitable shelter nearby. The vacant lot where she lived was an almost empty space aside from the big chestnut tree and tall grass. The matter was becoming urgent because the big day was not far off. Then she noticed it: right there, close to the massive iron gate at the entrance to the vacant lot, a young fir tree with branches hanging low. It was the perfect place! Well, there were some pros and cons. On the positive side, the vacant lot was fenced off, and even the gate was closed with a big padlock. Humans wouldn't be able to enter, which was good. So far, she has only had bad experiences with humans. Sometimes they threw stones at her when she passed through their gardens, and sometimes they even asked their dogs to run after her!

But this little tree was so close to the street! It was almost leaning on the fence, and the busy, frightening street was just on the other side. Hmm, what to do? Frankly, the choices on the vacant lot were minimal, so she decided to visit the interior of the little property.

She bent down and crawled inside the branches. It was quite a cosy place! Not precisely Versailles, rather a modest one-bedroom studio with no kitchen or bathroom.

"How much is it?" she asked the tree, not knowing that trees don't talk. But they do sing! A light breeze blew through the branches, and they whispered a sweet melody:

"It's nothing, my dear—this tree is for free!" At least that's what it sounded like to her. So often we hear what we want to hear.

"Merci!" she cried, for she was a French cat.

She skipped over the tall grass with a light tread, searching for nursery equipment. She found loads of dry leaves under the chestnut tree that she could use to make a bed; then, she collected some moss from Mrs Martin's garden to soften the leaves.

And oh, what a bargain! She spotted a pair of woollen gloves on Peter's terrace that the old man had put out to dry and then forgot to pick up. Perfect for wrapping babies in! That way, they wouldn't be cold at night, and Peter certainly had lots of other gloves – this pair was very old but valuable anyway. It was a complicated item to take with her, but she managed to drag the gloves through the gardens and gradually into her new home.

All that was left now was to build a front door. Just across the street was a thick hedge. She braved the heavy traffic several times, and little by little, she brought back enough small twigs to hide the entrance to her tiny house. That was it! Once finished, her new home wasn't inferior to those modern buildings you see in posh architectural magazines.

Now that everything was ready, the kitty became impatient. How many kitties were there in her belly? One, two, a hundred? She had no idea.

One day, very early in the morning, she began to feel pain: her belly hurt so much that she became afraid. She left her little house under the tree and hid in the tall grass, curling upon herself. But the pain wouldn't go away; it was getting stronger and stronger. Suddenly she understood. Quickly, she ran back to her home, and by the time she lay down on her cosy, soft bed, I, Freddy, had come into the world! Yes, I was the first to emerge from my Maman's belly. I was so curious to see what the big wide world looked like! Time to say oh and ah, and sister Caramel arrived. Little minx that she is, she declared: "I was first! It's just that you pushed me at the end!

A Very Hot Spring

In the beginning, everything went smoothly, and our first days were beautiful. We drank the milk Maman offered us, cuddled up to her belly, and spent our days sleeping, buried in her soft fur. We grew fast, and after a week or so, Maman led us out to show us the world beyond our house. Phew, dear reader! I never imagined the world could be so big! And fenced on all sides! Only one thing frightened me: on the other side of the enormous gate was a track, and monsters streamed over it in all directions. They were going so fast! Faster than the speed of light, I swear! Our Maman said they were cars, and the track was a street. She told us we should never go near it under any circumstances.

We didn't need to, as playing on the vacant lot was so much fun. We jumped over the tall grass, played hide and seek, and chased each other. If only we weren't so hungry all the time. Our Maman would go out several times a day to find something to eat, but that spring the weather was boiling, and food was scarcer than gold. Even the supply of flies and worms came up short. Water, too, was sorely lacking. It hadn't rained for months, and all the puddles in the vacant lot dried up. Evening after evening, our poor Maman came back with nothing. What little she could find from time to time was for us, her kittens. We were only two weeks old but were already eating solid food because our Maman could hardly give us any more milk.

The situation was desperate, and events almost turned out tragically.

Exhausted, Yet So Brave

It had been a particularly tough week. For several days, we had nothing to eat and nothing to drink, and our Maman had no more milk left to offer us, not even a drop. Caramel became so poorly that she refused to leave the inside of our home. Maman was afraid for her, but she, too, was so weak that she wobbled and dragged her paws when she walked. I still had enough strength to chase flies; from time to time, I even managed to swallow one or bring it to Maman and Caramel. But soon, I too became too tired and stayed inside, curled up next to my sister.

One dreadfully hot afternoon, the three of us were lying inside our tiny home, unable to find the strength to get up. Caramel and I were snuggled up to Maman, and she was kissing us from time to time to cheer us up. I felt her desperation. I don't know how it was possible, but I could always feel what Maman felt, even when she was not near me.

Gathering her last strength, Maman decided to try searching for food one last time. "Don't move from the house," she said. "Just wait for me; I won't be long." And she wobbled away, her poor paws hardly able to carry her.

I remember it well – it was the longest afternoon of my life: I truly believed our Maman would never return. Later she told us how it went.

After more than an hour of wandering through the neighbouring gardens, our Maman had visited every place she knew. Yet she couldn't find any food. There wasn't a single crumb in front of the bakery. Neither were there any leftovers near the dustbins; there was nothing in the saucers of the neighbourhood cats, and even the dog bowls were hopelessly empty.

If only I could find something for the little ones, thought Maman. Poor little black kitty, so thin that we could have counted her ribs if we had known how to count, yet she cared only about the two of us. Even her once-shiny black coat had become dull and grey.

She had been walking around for hours, and the afternoon was almost ending. She had never ventured so far from the vacant lot before. She thought, *I should go back now, while my legs can still carry me. I'm usually back by now. The poor kids must be worried.* She imagined the two of us sitting by the gate, desperately calling for her. *They must be so impatient,* she thought. She felt her strength failing – would she even be able to return home? She stopped in front of a small wall at the end of a little garden;

she could see a paved path leading to a terrace on the other side. Should she try this last garden? She knew that jumping up on the wall would exhaust her, even though it was a low one. *I'll just look in this new garden, and then I'll go home*, she thought. So, she gathered all her remaining strength and jumped over, only to find herself in yet another unknown garden.

A vast bamboo hedge lined the paved pathway leading to the large terrace. *There may be some food on this terrace*, thought our Maman. She saw a fountain at the end of the path: fresh water! She hadn't had any for days, and she was so thirsty. *Quick*, she thought, *I can reach it, I can do it! I want to drink, drink!*

Sadly, her poor paws refused to carry her just those few steps further. Too weak to take even one more step, she collapsed halfway between the fountain and the terrace in the middle of the path.

She lay there on the warm flagstones, unable to get up and drag herself any further. *What will become of my darlings?* She wondered. *Who will take care of them if I don't return?* She was filled with sadness.

Maman knew she should meow, call for help. Maybe there was another cat in this garden that could help her. She thought of her neighbour, that vain Charlotte. If only she were close, she would be willing to help. And even that pirate Big Head, the gardens' bandit, would help. After all, wasn't he the kids' dad? Cats do help each other when needed. She tried to meow, but no sound came from her exhausted little body.

This is the end, she thought. *My little ones, my poor little ones! If only they were here, near me.* She closed her beautiful green eyes and sank into a coma-like sleep.

Dear reader, do you believe in miracles? I do!

For you see, the garden where our Maman was trespassing belonged to Mum. Yes, the very Mum who was to pick me up off the pavement one stormy night a few weeks later. But a lot would happen in the meantime.

I'll let Mum tell you how she first met our Maman. She knows the story better.

Life Hanging by a Thin Thread

I remember my first meeting with the little black kitty very well. It was a hot April afternoon. I was working in my home office on the first floor when suddenly I saw a small black shape in the garden, creeping along the path. It was moving with great difficulty as if each step forward were a challenge. It frequently stopped, sat down to regain strength, and resumed its slow walk towards the terrace. Looking closer, I saw that it was a cat: a tiny black kitty. Suddenly, the little kitty collapsed on her side, stretching out her legs and lying motionless.

At first, I was afraid she was dead, but then I realised that she might just be utterly exhausted. I rushed to the kitchen to fill a bowl with cat food and another with fresh water. Once in the garden, I approached her slowly, trying not to make any noise. Had she noticed my presence? She showed no sign of it: her little body remained motionless, and her ears did not twitch. I called her softly – I was close to her now. Her fur was dull and dirty, and one of her hind legs seemed hurt; a trickle of dried blood was visible. She was skinny, and I thought it must have been long since her last meal. I put the two bowls close to her head and drew back a few steps.

I don't know how long I waited, but it was long enough to get me worried. Just as I had decided to fetch a basket and take her to the vet, she raised her tiny, skinny head, looked up at me and opened her mouth, probably to greet me with a meow. But no sound came out. She was so weak that even her voice had failed her.

"Poor baby," I said, "my little darling, eat a little. Look, I brought you some delicious food!" She raised her head to the bowl's height and caught a couple of cat biscuits. After swallowing them with difficulty, she got up by folding her front legs under her body. In this uncomfortable position, she started eating biscuit after biscuit with long intervals between bites. Any hungry cat would have pounced on the food and emptied the bowl. But this poor kitty was so exhausted that even eating was a task beyond her strength.

That day, her life was hanging by a fragile thread. Had I not seen her, she would have stayed there, lying on our garden's paved path, sinking little by little into unconsciousness and then into noth-ingness.

A good quarter of an hour later, with some more biscuits swallowed, she had enough energy to sit up properly and eat and drink with more spirit.

That day, she stayed in our garden for over two hours. She kept eating little by little, then resting again. I was so happy to have rescued her that I kept running into the kitchen, looking for good things to offer her. Ham, leftover chicken, a bowl of milk, treats – whatever I thought would please her. There was plenty of cat food at my house to feed my seven Maine Coons. They weren't allowed into the garden but could come to the patio. Curiously, on that day, and probably because it was so hot, they all slept inside.

It had started to get dark when she finally decided that her belly was full enough. She rummaged in her plate and carefully picked out the most prominent remaining piece of ham, holding it tightly in her mouth. She looked at me as if to say thank you, turned around, and slowly started to walk towards the low wall from where she had probably come. Carrying the piece of ham was not easy; she often stopped to put it on the ground and rest a little before picking it up again and continuing on her way.

It was evident that this kitty had little kittens some-where. But where?

I followed her progress, trying to spot her tiny body here and there while she slipped from garden to garden, hedge to hedge, but it was difficult to make out her black shape as the darkness descended. All I could do was hope she would return the next day for more food.

* * *

Here ends Mum's telling of the story. As for us, to our utmost delight, Maman came home later in the evening with a piece of ham. I don't know who was happiest – Caramel and I, as we finally got something to eat, or Maman as she watched us gobbling up our small dinner!

We thought that happy times had finally come for us. Maman had found a place to get food, and the weather cooled slightly. We played and jumped and ran around, as happy as can be. We chased butterflies, napped under the chestnut tree, and cuddled with our Maman. Happiness reigned on the vacant lot – our kingdom and I thought nothing unpleasant would ever happen again. I was partly right. Indeed, for a short while, life did improve.

But after a couple of blissful weeks, disaster struck. Again.

Yellow Monster

A Few Happy Weeks

Of course, the piece of ham that Maman brought that evening wasn't enough for two starving kittens, but we enjoyed it so much! We hadn't had anything to eat for days. We asked for more; however, we understood that Maman was too tired to look for more food that evening. So we curled up next to her inside our tiny home under the fir tree and fell asleep.

The following morning, Maman told us she had discovered a magic garden where a lovely lady served as much food as one could ever desire. To eat as much as we want? What wonderful news! We were so happy!

Although it was still early, Maman decided that she had to return to that magic garden. As soon as we were awake, she washed us quickly, then said: "*Petits* (she used to call us *petits* as a sign of affection), please go and sit in the sunny spot on the grass over there and wait for me. I'll fetch your breakfast. I won't be long this time."

"Oh, can we play, Maman?" I asked because, you know, sitting still has always been difficult for me.

"Yes, but no wild games! And don't go into the street – don't even approach the gate!"

We promised, then watched our mother slip between the gate bars, cross the street and disappear into the opposite hedge. My sister asked: "Is she back yet?"

"Silly, she just left!" I replied and started to tease her.

That day, Maman returned to the magic garden at least five times! "Oh, my darlings," she told us, "That lady is so kind! As soon as she sees me, she hurries to the kitchen and brings something for me even if there are plenty of cat biscuits on the garden table! She must know I have kittens because she is careful to offer me food that I can carry away."

We listened with open mouths and marvelled, "Oh, Maman, please can we go with you to the garden?"

"Not yet, my chickens, but soon! A few weeks more, and then you'll be big enough to cross the street and follow me." We didn't mind; we were so happy on our vacant lot! The more we grew, the more frequent Maman's visits to the magic garden became, and she never returned without a little something for us.

But soon, the amount of food Maman could carry had become too small to satisfy the appetites of two fast-growing kittens. Of course, these comings and goings were exhausting for her and dangerous. We worried about her every time we saw her standing on the pavement on the other side of the big gate, ready to leave. She would look to the left, then to the right, waiting for the traffic to clear enough to cross between two roaring monsters. It was so frightening! And the time she was away seemed so long! But we were always delighted when we spotted her frail silhouette emerging from the hedge on the other side of the road. Even when it happened ten times a day, every time I wanted to dance, jump as high as the sky and run around in circles as soon as she returned. Caramel and I always remembered the day when she nearly didn't come back, so we couldn't help fearing for her life.

Then, one day, something happened that ended those dangerous comings and goings.

The lady from the magic garden knew that our Maman had kittens somewhere – she had seen her taking the food away from the first day on. But she couldn't find us. The gardens in the neighbourhood followed one another in a row, and hedges of cypresses divided them. Our Maman, anxious not to be followed, would tread her way through this vegetation. It was impossible to see her: once she had crossed one or two of the neighbouring gardens, she had disappeared among the leaves and branches.

So, the kind lady asked her nearest neighbour if he could look in his hedges – the kittens' home might be hidden there.

"Oh yes, madame," he replied, "I'll look immediately! They must not be allowed to grow. How would we get rid of them afterwards?"

You can easily imagine how that upset the lady! She wanted so much to save us and wished she could help our Maman with all her heart! Forgetting restraint and politeness, she asked the neighbour not to try looking and then continued searching for us as much as she could. However, the houses were protected by high fences, making it impossible to see what was happening behind them. The number of places she could visit was limited. And she never imagined that we lived so far away from her house. But I'll let her tell you what happened next.

An Incredible Chance

That afternoon, my son and I were returning from a shopping centre – we had bought some interesting books and were discussing our future reading in the car. My son was driving.

Then suddenly, not far from our house, I caught a glimpse of a tiny black and white kitten sitting on the pavement in front of a vacant lot. I shouted, "Stop! Stop!"

My son braked sharply. It was late afternoon, and the traffic was very dense – the car behind us almost hit us. Naturally, my son was upset: I shouldn't have shouted so loudly. He was right, but I was so excited! I was sure the little creature on the pavement was one of the kittens I had been looking for.

It was strange to see such a tiny kitten sitting on the pavement while cars were speeding past him – how fearless he was! But would he run away if I got close? I stepped out of the car and walked slowly toward the kitten. I was just a few steps away when he noticed me, hesitated, and then slipped back to the vacant lot.

He wasn't alone – another little kitten was sitting in the sun-baked grass inside the gate. This one was a tabby with white paws. I looked around for the mother – were these the little black kitty's kids? Many feral cats wandered around our area: it's very green, with gardens and a big park nearby – the perfect environment for street cats.

I didn't have to wait long. All at once, my little black friend appeared from across the street. She was carrying a piece of bacon in her mouth – I had put some bacon on a small plate in the garden before I'd left in case she came for food during my absence. Can you imagine how happy I was, how excited? I ran all the way home. Naturally, my son had gone to park the car in the meantime.

Once in the kitchen, I filled a large bowl with cat biscuits, grabbed a milk bottle, filled saucers and small plates with roast chicken leftovers, and then headed back to the vacant lot.

That evening, the kittens and their mother were given a sumptuous feast!

The next day, and for more than a week, I visited the vacant lot twice a day – in the morning and late in the evening – and each time it was a celebration, a banquet.

I would stand in front of the kitty's home on the pavement as it was impossible to go inside the vacant lot due to the padlock on the gate. If the kitties weren't in sight, I would call them. The one who always came first was the little black and white, the little guy from the pavement –actually you, my Freddy. You would answer my calls with tiny, happy mews and then bounce through the tall grass with little jumps. Several years later, I can still see you, a lovely little boy, running up to the big iron gate to greet me. But you always stayed inside the vacant lot, too far away for me to cuddle or touch you.

I didn't mind, though. I was delighted to have found the kittens, to be able to bring them food and to see how happy they were.

Sometimes during the day, I would stop my car in front of the vacant lot if I came back from shopping and had something in my basket that the kitties might like. Sometimes I would even sit on a stone next to the gate and talk to them.

People passing by must have thought I was crazy, but I didn't mind: those were blissful moments for the little cat family and me. I thought of the day when I could take them to my garden and tried to figure out how I could do that. For the moment, they were still too small and needed their mother. I wasn't sure she would follow them once I had taken them to my house. And they were so happy here that it hurt my heart to think of uprooting them.

It was just a vacant lot, but to them, it was paradise.

The kittens were out of danger now, I thought. A few weeks ago, I'd saved their mother when she arrived half dead in my garden; the little ones would not have survived without her. Now, I had found them and cared for them. Innocently I believed that by saving them twice, so to speak, I had somehow earned the right to a happy outcome. All the difficulties were behind us.

But they weren't, far from it.

Terrible Shock

One sunny morning, I was having a busy day in my home office, and I couldn't go to the vacant lot as early as usual. A little before noon, I could finally pack a food bag for the kitties. Then I hurried to them, walking with light steps, looking forward to seeing my babies again. My house was full of cats with my seven Maine Coons, but these little kittens on the vacant lot had become my special treasure. I loved them more than anything.

As I approached the kitties' home, I heard the sound of heavy equipment at work. I thought they were mending a road, or maybe there was maintenance work in progress in the nearby park. A bit worried, I walked faster ...

Oh, what a shock when I finally saw the vacant lot! How dreadful! I stopped, totally stunned. The fence had been knocked down, and a big yellow machine was digging a massive hole in the middle of the lot. Already, piles of earth had been excavated and massed all around. I'm not an expert on construction equipment so I couldn't name it precisely, but I think the digging machine was a bulldozer. It must have been at work since the early morning hours, given the vast amount of earth it had already moved.

The noise was deafening. Where were my little family, the mother and her kittens? The fir tree, their "home" lay pitifully close to the big gate, its roots in the air. Why did the workers need to dig it up? They were digging the hole in the middle of the vacant lot, far from the kitties' home. They had put a big sign at the entrance that said "Worksite Closed to Public," but I stepped inside anyway.

It was not easy to make progress between the chips and clods of earth. I had to climb mounds of the soil before reaching the devilish yellow machine. It was useless to try to speak or even shout: the noise was too loud. So, I just waited there, holding my little basket of cat food, hoping the workers would notice me. After a time, they did.

Greeting them with the usual *bonjour* and my best smile, I asked: "Did you see a black cat or kittens when you arrived?"

"No, ma'am, we haven't seen anything."

"Have you been here for long?"

"Yes, since dawn."

"And you are sure you haven't seen any cats?"

"No, no, there were no cats on this property."

"Oh. Please take my phone number, and by all means, give me a call if you see a black cat or small kittens. I'll reward you!"

The workers consented, but I doubted they would pay attention to the cats. Anyway, the noise here was such that it would have frightened any living creature. Even the birds had flown away.

They allowed me to walk here and there on the lot and search around the fences, but I knew it was useless. There was an office building opposite the vacant lot with a security guard. I asked him the same questions: had he seen any cats around? He might have seen which way they ran. But, no, he hadn't. I again left my phone number. I rang the doorbells of the nearest houses, and some owners allowed me to search their gardens. I left my phone number everywhere, and by the end of the afternoon, the whole neighbourhood knew me and had my mobile phone number.

However, all my searching was fruitless.

I realised that the vacant lot was actually a lot with an owner who had decided to build a house. The black kitty and her kittens had lost their home forever, and it was high time to take them to my garden, where they would be safe, well-fed and loved. But first, they had to be found.

I returned to the vacant lot several times that evening. I even went there in the middle of the night, hoping the kitties would come back for food. But no matter how long I waited, whether I called for them or left them food, there wasn't even a slender sign of the little family. No sound, no rustling in the bushes. The food was eaten during the night, but how to know who had taken advantage of the free meal? Many stray cats and even foxes from the park wandered around.

What had happened to the kittens and their mother? Where were they? I kept looking, exploring the surroundings every day and questioning the neighbours. But no one saw the kittens. They had vanished.

I let Freddy explain what happened, as it's a mystery to me.

Dreadful Days

It was the most terrible day of my life and will always remain in my memory. That morning shaped my whole life. Mum said it "traumatised" me – whatever that means.

It was still very early and we were asleep, curled next to Maman in our tiny house under the fir tree. I dreamed I was chasing a butterfly at the far end of the vacant lot; it was so much fun that I was laughing aloud. But then a bee came and started circling my head, closer and closer to my ears, buzzing more and more loudly. Annoyed, I tried to slap to make it go away, but it only got louder. The noise became deafening, unbearable even.

It hammered in my head – it was hurting me! It was no longer one bee but a hundred, a thousand, ten thousand bees! I grew frightened. I woke up and saw Maman leaning over me. She touched me with her paw: "Freddy, run, hide! We're in grave danger! Freddy! Caramel! Follow me!"

And without waiting for us, she leapt out, sure we would follow her.

I ran out just in time to catch a glimpse of Maman disappearing at the far end of the lot. She had climbed up the big chestnut tree and jumped over the high wall bordering the grounds' northern part.

"Come on, Caramel!" I shouted and started to run, too frightened to wait for my sister. *She's going to follow me*, I thought. On the right side, I saw a terrible yellow monster not far from our house. It was invading the whole lot, encroaching on it, crushing everything in its way, roaring like mad!

I ran as fast as I could, and I could run fast. I would win all the speed races if there were a Cat Olympics.

"Freddy, wait!" cried Caramel, but I didn't. I was so scared that I simply couldn't stop running.

I did what Maman had done and climbed the giant tree, but I fell to the ground trying to jump over the wall. I didn't even know whether I had hurt myself: the terror inside me had submerged all other feelings. I just started to crawl in the opposite direction. On the west side, a simple fence bordered the vacant lot. Was there a hole through which I could escape? Unable to find one, I tried to dig into the ground, but it was so hard that all I managed to do was to hurt my paws. There was nothing else to do than to crawl further to the big iron gate through which our Maman used to sneak when she went to fetch our dinner. I remembered that she always looked left and right before crossing the street, but I had no time for this. I only dashed– I didn't care if there were cars. The horrible roaring monster was so close, the noise so horrifying, that I was ready to risk my life to escape it.

I ran across the street, crossed a lawn and another large street, and ended up in a park. The terrible noise was still in the air but coming from afar and less threatening. In front of me, I saw a space where the trees grew so tall and close that it was almost dark beneath them. *This is a friendly area,* I thought and I stepped inside. The ground was covered with a carpet of pine needles, perfect for my aching paws, so I decided to explore a bit. And oh, what a chance find

I came across! A hole in the ground, a burrow next to a tree, seemed empty. I crawled inside, rolled up into a ball, and hoped this house had no owner. My heart was beating so fast that I thought it would leap out of my body. I was shaking all over; my ribs hurt from the fall, and my claws were bruised. But curled in that tiny burrow, I managed to calm down bit by bit and soon fell asleep, too tired to think about anything.

I woke in complete darkness. I had probably slept the whole day. Where was Maman? Where was Caramel? Had they managed to escape the danger? I knew I should go back to our tiny home. I felt guilty for having left Caramel behind. Dear reader, call me a wimp if you want, but I must confess that I didn't dare to move that night. Nor the next day.

Besides, early in the morning, the noise came back. Off in the distance, of course, but it was there. Who knows, the yellow monster could have decided to go after me at any moment!

It was only late the second night, when all was silent again, that I dared to leave my retreat. I felt too hungry to wait any longer: I had to find food.

I crept back to the vacant lot. What desolation! Our tiny home had been knocked down, and oh, imagine!

The ground where we used to run and chase each other was now full of strange hills, slopes and holes! Did nature itself also want to harm us? I felt as if the whole world had become unfriendly and hated us.

I called for Maman and Caramel. First, there was no reply. But as I kept calling, I heard a meow in the distance. Caramel! My sister has a distinctive voice that can be recognised among millions.

I called her name and within seconds saw her running towards me. We rubbed against each other, we kissed, we cuddled, and I asked her ten questions at a time: "Where have you been? Where is Maman? Are you all right?"

"Oh Freddy, I couldn't find Maman anywhere! I hid over there in a garden, inside a pile of wood."

My poor sister sobbed while she spoke, and I had to give her nose kisses and head rubs until she calmed down.

"Don't worry, Sis, now that we are together, we'll find Maman! And don't get lost again – if I start running, follow me, don't linger behind!"

She promised, and we started exploring the ground around the gate – in case the lady from the magic garden had left some food for us. But all we found was an upturned saucer and a few cat biscuits scattered here and there. Still, it was something, so we swallowed them greedily.

A Storm Monster

We wanted to start searching our surroundings: we had to find our Maman! But suddenly, something terrible happened. The noise again! This time it came from above, from the sky. A horrible, thundering, relentless noise invaded the night. A monster was spitting fire across the sky! I was sure it was that same yellow monster: the one from the vacant lot. It had invaded the sky! Later I learned it was a storm monster. We were so afraid! It has decided to swallow us both. Where could we go?

We started to run. We looked for a place to escape, but no matter which direction we went, the monster was always just above our heads, following our every step. The whole night had become a giant demon – this was the end for us! We ran to the left, to the right, towards the north, then the south. But nothing stopped the rumbling; there was no way out of the dreadful night.

Finally, I don't know how we ended up in the garden where Caramel had hidden before and crawled inside a pile of logs.

How long did we stay there? One, two, three days? More? I couldn't tell. As I later learned, the storm continued for three days and nights. They say it was one of the biggest and longest storms ever seen around Paris.

After a time that felt endless, we became so hungry that we decided to venture back to the big gate on the vacant lot. Maybe we would find some more biscuits scattered on the ground? Perhaps we had overlooked some?

Outside the wood pile, the rain was falling heavily. But when we listened, the awful noise wasn't there anymore. The monster had seemingly retreated. Was it just hiding, waiting for us to show up so it could jump on us? Possibly – we had to remain extra careful.

Exhausted, we dragged our shivering bodies to the gate. We hadn't eaten for so long! If only we could find a little something: a crumb, anything! But regardless of how hard we looked, how carefully we searched, there was not a single soggy cat biscuit left in the mud around the gate.

36

Suddenly I had an idea. "Caramel, you know what? Do you remember the day I went to sit on the pavement? I was looking for Maman to return, and suddenly the lady from the magic garden appeared, and we were so happy after that?"

"Oh yes, Freddy! And she brought us plenty of food! Maybe you should go and sit on the pavement again? Maybe she'll come?" Poor Caramel was thrilled at the idea.

I thought it very unlikely, but what did we have to lose? It was worth a try.

Here, I'll let Mum share what happened next.

* * *

Telepathic Communication

It had been five or six days since I had seen either the little kittens or their mother. The construction works continued on the former vacant lot.

Moreover, it had rained constantly over the previous few days. Big thunderstorms had raged above our heads, and no sooner had one storm ended than another was on the horizon. The rumblings and lightning bolts were so frequent and violent that even my bold Maine Coons had lived in hiding places most of those days.

Given the horrible weather, it was improbable that the little family would have returned to the vacant lot.

I hoped that they had remained together, that the kittens were with their mother. I also hoped that she would bring them to my garden. She knew where I was, where the food supply was. Before I started delivering food to the vacant lot, she used to come to my house several times a day. Why didn't she come now?

Despite my most fervent hopes, she didn't make an appearance. Nor did she return to the vacant lot. Every evening, I went to their former home and called for her and her tiny family. I'd wait, then call again, but in vain.

I would go out several times a night, wearing my boots and raincoat in the pouring rain, in the frightening storms. I would go with my little bag full of cat food, hopeful on the way there, desperate on the way back.

One memorable evening, despite the heavy rain, I had already gone to the vacant lot three times to check for the kitties. My last visit happened around eleven and, again, I couldn't find anyone; nobody was answering my calls. Sad and desperate, I returned home. Where were they? Were they still alive? Had they found a shelter and something to eat or were they wandering around, hopeless and starving?

By chance, I had a lot of work in my home office, which distracted me from my sadness.

Then suddenly, in the middle of a task, a thought flashed across my mind: *they are there! Now, at this very moment!* I checked my watch – it was well past midnight, almost 1 a.m. As I listened to the rain drumming on the windows, I got ready: boots, a rain-coat, small bag of cat food. Despite the fact, that I thought I was crazy to go out in such weather and at such a late hour, I had to go.

It was a hunch, a feeling, an intangible emergency call – a telepathic communication.

As I approached, I noticed a small white shape on the pavement right in front of the vacant lot in the dark of the night. Was it just a piece of white paper? Was it a cat? I sped my pace up. The little shape moved and disappeared into the night, and I knew it: it was one of them, one of my kittens!

BABY FREDDY

Two Tiny Kittens on the Pavement

"Is she coming yet?" asked Caramel.

A bit annoyed, I turned to her. She's always so impatient, wanting things to happen at once! But the sight of her little skinny body shivering in the rain made me feel sorry. I would do anything to help her!

"She'll come, don't worry," I replied, not believing it myself.

I waited, though I felt exhausted, cold and hungry. It was raining more and more, and I could barely see anything in the distance. I considered returning to our refuge in the pile of logs with my sister.

But oh, wait! Was that the shape of a person in the curtain of rain? It was moving, approaching fast. Could it be her, the lady from the magic garden? Was she bringing us food? Hesitant and a bit frightened, I slipped between the gate bars back to the vacant lot, to my sister. Just a few seconds later, she was standing in front of us. And she seemed so happy!

"Babies, my little darlings! Finally, here you are!" she exclaimed and started to unpack her small bag. "My poor babies, you must be so hungry! Come, I've brought you lots of delicious things to eat. You'll like them!"

She pulled out a plate and filled it with cat biscuits and ham. We waited impatiently in the mud, our tongues licking our lips and our mouths salivating. Food! I wanted to jump forward and eat, eat, eat! Only, there was a problem: the plate was on the wrong side of the gate! The lady had placed it on the pavement, not our vacant lot! I had never been up close to her or any other human. Maman had told us they could be dangerous.

Yet our dinner was waiting at the feet of the lady from the magic garden! Was she dangerous, too? Ah, if only Maman were here. I'm sure she would bring the food to us like she used to! I was perplexed. This was torture! That food so near and yet so far ... I felt so scared, yet so hungry! I didn't look at my sister, but I could feel her shaking with anticipation, her body firmly pressed against mine. Suddenly, without further thought, I dashed out onto the pavement. The call of the food, the hunger, had overtaken my mind.

My sister immediately followed me, and together we started gobbling the delicious dinner, our first meal in many, many days.

Then something terrible happened. All at once, just when we were beginning to enjoy food, the lady bent down and grabbed us both!

Dear reader, this was a betrayal! The type of treachery of which only a human is capable! Maman had told us to beware of humans, so I should have known better. I hoped my sister would manage to slip from her hand and run away. I heard her screaming, calling me, meowing. Still, I was held firmly, unable to free myself no matter how hard I twitched, squirmed and wiggled. Before I knew it, I found myself inside a tightly closed handbag with just enough air to breathe. Of course, I fought, banging around inside the tiny space. I cried and meowed; I called Maman and Caramel for help, and I clawed that stupid bag as hard as possible, hoping it would rip open. But it didn't.

Then, before I could understand what was happening to me, I was out!

Yes! The handbag had opened to let in bright light! I was so dizzy that, at first, I didn't move. What was this new space around me? Had the world shrunk in such a short time? Later I learned Mum released me in the hallway and closed the door leading further into the house. But there was no time for deep thinking: I had to get out of there! I jumped to the ground and started to run. But how strange! I had taken only a few steps when my head hit something hard – a wall! I ran in the opposite direction, and the same thing happened, a wall again! And a glass door. Then another one! It seemed as if this world was made up of doors and walls, and no matter how much I hit them with my head, none of them would give way!

My head started aching. I was lost; I couldn't even remember how I got into this strange place. Then someone picked me up. I was so scared that I closed my eyes. But a familiar smell reached my nostrils, a gentle warmth enfolded me, and I recalled everything. It was her, the lady from the magic garden, who always arrived with food when we were hungry, who talked to us so gently – the one who had brought me here.

I had no reason to be scared anymore. I decided to kiss her on her neck. And once again on her nose and one more time on her cheek. She kissed me back, and then it was tit for tat: we swapped one, two, three, a hundred kisses! I knew I was safe, and she was my Mum. This strange space with doors and walls was a tiny part of my new shelter, and at first sight, it already seemed far better than the pile of logs or the burrow in the park.

Mum dried my fur, offered me warm milk and a plate of ham, and installed me in a cosy basket.

"Sleep well," she said, "I'm going back now to look for your sister." And she left.

But I wasn't frightened anymore. My belly was full, and I felt happy and comfy in the basket, wrapped in soft blankets. I fell asleep. I did not doubt that my sister would be with me when I woke up.

But it didn't happen that way, at least not for a long time.

I'll let Mum tell you more. She knows this part better.

Looking for Caramel

That same night, I returned to the vacant lot, trying to find the second kitten. The rain had stopped, the sky was starting to clear up, and even a few stars lit up the sky. A good omen, I thought, just to cheer me on. I had little hope of finding Freddy's sister immediately – she had probably been too frightened to come back after what had happened. However, I hoped she would at least have come back during my absence to finish her dinner. With disappointment, I saw that the plate was still full of food. She hadn't even dared come back for a few more bites! Despite the late hour, I stayed on the pavement for quite a long time, calling softly. In vain. I thought that the kitten would probably come back the following night or in a couple of days and I returned home, happy that I'd managed to save at least one of them. I was sure the tabby kitten knew I would keep coming back at night and would show up sooner or later.

The next day, I took Freddy to the vet. He got his vaccinations, and the vet rid him of ticks and fleas. The kitten, he said, although a bit too thin, was in good health.

Back home, I introduced Freddy to my seven Maine Coons. They were my little family of cats: Mummy,

Daddy, their four daughters, and the uncle of the gang, the oldest one. To tell the truth, I had never wanted to have so many cats – one little ball of fur to love, to cherish, to care for was enough for me. Little did I know that my seven Maine Coons were only the beginning and that very soon, there would be fifteen cats and sometimes more settling either in my house or in my garden! But more about that later – let's get back to Freddy's arrival.

I was slightly concerned that Freddy would be afraid of my giant Maine Coons, so I stayed close, ready to "save" him. But what happened was precisely the opposite. It was an enchanting scene. The tiny kitten went from one Maine Coon to another, then bent his head and stuffed it under their chins between their paws, waiting to be licked. After he had received a tongue brushing, he rubbed his cheek against each one and moved to another Maine Coon to repeat the performance. They all welcomed him warmly.

I felt guilty for letting Caramel escape from my hands – I had been holding her! How had she managed to slip away? And why had she not come back for food? But I continued going to the vacant lot night after night. I would call and wait, sometimes for a long time. It was more complicated now: the landowner had erected high fences around the lot and barricaded the big gate with boards. I couldn't see what was happening inside. It became impossible to slide a saucer under the gate for the little one if she came looking for food. The only option was to leave a small heap of cat biscuits on the side of the pavement, but they were always just scattered around the next day. Where could she be? It was unlikely that she had strayed far – she seemed much more fearful than Freddy and always used to stay behind him.

I started my neighbourhood investigation again, knocking on doors and disturbing the neighbours.

"Have you seen a little kitten roaming around here? Could you please look thoroughly at your garden? Under the bushes, inside the hedges? Would you, please? Oh, wonderful! A thousand thanks!"

Again, I left my mobile phone number everywhere. What a shame I had never taken any pictures of the kittens on the vacant lot! I was now unable to show anyone what Caramel looked like.

All my searching remained fruitless. Then one day, a neighbour told me that a lady at the bakery had mentioned having found a little starved kitten on the pavement and taking it home. The neighbour didn't know the woman and could not say where she lived or what colour that kitten was. As there likely weren't many starving kittens wandering around, I was pretty sure it must have been Freddy's sister.

However, only a few days later, I heard desperate meows in my garden. It was Caramel's voice! She has a distinctive voice – you can't mistake her for any other cat. I rushed outside and caught a glimpse of her tiny face in the rhododendron bush. She looked terrified. She retreated further into the flower bed with every step I took forward.

I hurried back to the kitchen to get some food. I thought a bit of ham or leftover chicken would bring her out of her hiding place. But by the time I returned, she had disappeared. I called, searched, and watched for hours, hoping she would come back.

Once again, my hopes were vain.

After that unexpected meeting that only lasted the briefest moment, I felt deeply depressed. When I spotted the kitten in the flower bed, my heart leapt with joy, and an immense pleasure flooded me. I felt so relieved to see her again! I thought she came to stay with us; I thought she would remain here, with her brother and me. But it wasn't to be – not yet, at least. My feelings and my bond with these two kittens went beyond all logic. Was it because I was convinced that I was their only hope?

We didn't see Caramel for a long time after that first sighting. Yet someone else came back. I'll let Freddy tell you who.

Startling Reception

I should have been the happiest of cats now. I had a new family. I had two Mums (my Mummy Maine Coon, named Tahiti, and my human Mum) and even two Daddies (my Daddy Maine Coon, called Uddy, and a human Dad)! Everyone loved me, and I loved everyone. I played, raced from room to room, rushed up and down the stairs, lazed around on the patio when the weather was fine and slept on the soft beds on rainy days. I had plenty of delicious food at my disposal and a thousand toys. Any cat would have been delighted to be so pampered and loved.

But I'll tell you a secret: I would have preferred to be outside, in our tiny house under the fir tree, with my beautiful Maman and my sister Caramel. I missed them so much!

A glass front door in my new home led to a veranda from where I could see stray cats coming to claim their dinner in the evenings. I would sit there and keep watch – maybe one day my Maman would come too? She must be starving by now! I knew this was the house where she used to come for food when we were little; it had the same warm smell, and it looked the way she described it in her tales. So why didn't she come now? Would she ever come? How desperate I was to see her again! I dreamt that she would be there, just on the other side of the glass door, and I would leap towards her and kiss her, and we would hug and be so happy! I can't count the number of times I dreamt she was close to me, holding me, embracing me with her paws!

And you know what? One evening, I suddenly saw her little black head just in front of me, on the other side of the glass door! She didn't notice me: she was eating hastily from a plate because she must have been starved. I banged on the glass with my paws and my nose. I jumped in the air and called "Maman, Maman, Maman!" as loud as possible. I yelled and screamed. I scratched the glass, rolled on the floor, and cried. I cried so hard that Mum came running and when she understood what was happening, she had tears in her eyes.

"My little boy," she said, "you can't go out! You'll want to follow your Maman, and you'll be lost again!"

But I sobbed and howled and lamented so much that at last, Mum let me go out to greet my Maman. I dashed out as soon as she opened the door. I rolled at Maman's paws, just under her chin. I told her all the words of love I knew: "Maman darling, Maman, my little Maman! I love you; I love you so much, Maman!"

Then something strange happened. Instead of a kiss, a nice word, or a cuddle, my Maman gave me a big slap. She didn't seem to recognise me anymore.

"Go away!" she exclaimed and scratched my head.

Bewildered, I cried, "It's me, Maman! I'm your Freddy, dear Maman – I love you!"

But she looked at me with angry eyes, pulled my ears, pushed me away with her paws, hit me again, and furiously bit my back. I was so stunned that I remained crouched on the ground, unable to move.

Suddenly I heard Mum shouting, "No!" She jumped forward, picked me up, and took me back into the house, cuddling me.

Mum and I remained like this, cuddling for more than an hour. I sobbed on her lap, and Mum kept kissing me and holding me tight. She explained that my Maman loved me, but she knew I had to stay here, in my new home. It's a lovely home, and I'm cared for, loved – I'm a little prince. That's what Maman always wished for me, and she's happy to know I'm here. So, I mustn't follow her. I have to stay. Mum told me that Maman had wanted me to understand this when she bit me. She scratched me because she wanted the best possible future for me, but she truly loved me.

I understood every word Mum said, and the next time my Maman came to dine, I just said "Hello Maman" through the glass door and wandered away to play with Uddy, my new Daddy cat.

My Sister's Arrival

It was one summer afternoon that I spotted her. I was playing in the garden, trying to catch a butterfly, when suddenly I saw a shape, a tiny form, under Mum's car. As I approached, I was not only able to see that it was a cat but also what cat it was.

"Caramel?" I cried. "Sis, have you finally come?"

"Freddy!" My sister wanted to come towards me, to greet me, but she hadn't enough strength. She collapsed before she could get out. I called for Mum by meowing very loudly. She came running out of the house, believing that something terrible had happened to me, but I showed her Caramel. Mum went to her knees, reached under the car, and managed to pull my sister out.

Caramel was in such bad shape! She was half as big as me because she hadn't gotten enough food to grow. Her fur was dirty, full of mud and dust, and someone had put a collar so tightly around her neck that it was strangling her. I wondered how she was still able to breathe. I kissed her and then let Mum take her inside. My sister needed urgent help.

I didn't see her again that day. Mum took her to the vet, and Caramel had to stay there for "observation." I wasn't sure what that meant. After a day, she came back, and we were finally able to celebrate! We sat at the garden table, ready for a feast. Mum brought us plates of food, an assortment of the best she had in the fridge: tuna, roast chicken leftovers, treats, cat milk, cat biscuits and even ice cream! What a treat! We sat for hours and told each other everything that had happened while we were apart. Caramel told us a lousy family had adopted her; they had kept her closed up in a small room and often forgot to bring her food. The family's kids had mistreated her. Finally, they had dumped her back on the street, so she had wandered around looking for me.

My sister remains deeply affected by what happened to her while we were apart. Despite Mum's best efforts, she refuses to enter the house or stay inside. She has a deep fear of closed spaces and strangers and is afraid of other cats, especially Mum's giant Maine Coons. Yet they are so gentle and happy when they meet a new friend!

As a result, Mum arranged for her to live in the garden in as much comfort as possible. For example, Caramel feels safe when she is perched on the windowsill of the garage, so Mum lined the ledge with soft felt. My sister spends whole days resting on it, only coming down to eat or sleep. From her "refuge," she talks endlessly to Mum and me when-ever we come to keep her company – and we come often! At night, she creeps into the garage through a half-open window and further into the workshop, where she has a dedicated and safe place to sleep. I have tried to get her to come with us so many times, join us while we watch the hedges, explore the surroundings, and play catch-me-if-you-can, just like we used to on our vacant lot! She always refuses. Mum said we should let her live her own life as she wants it. What's important is that she is finally with us and happy. My sister has grown into a shiny, beau-tiful, large cat from the tiny, dirty kitten I spotted under Mum's car! She's almost bigger than me! At least, that's what Mum says, and it makes me a bit jealous.

I still hope that Caramel will be able to come into the house without panicking and nap with me on Mum's bed one day.

Mum herself is pleased to have us both with her. She says she has never had cats for which she searched so much, experienced so much despair, and yearned and hoped for so much!

Our Maman also comes to eat in the garden from time to time. But one day, she guessed that Mum was planning to trap her and take her to the vet to "spay" her. She disappeared for several weeks. When she finally returned, her belly was all round with new kitties – my brothers and sisters, said Mum. But that's a story for another chapter.

A French saying states: All's well that ends well. All well? Not quite! The Yellow Storm Monster is still around!

It still looks for us from time to time when it remembers us. Sometimes we'll be napping, hanging out, or eating, and it'll come out of nowhere.

"Where are they?" it thunders from the sky. "Where are that Freddy and his sister? I want to gobble them up!"

And then it sends lightning bolts across the sky to see us better. Between you and me, I think it must be a bit short-sighted, but don't tell it I said that! When it comes, I hide under Mum's bed, or better still, on top of the cupboard in the dressing room. Ha! It'll never find me there!

And besides, we have nothing to fear now. We're Mum's kids.

FREDDY IN HIS FOREVER HOME

Chapter Two

In which Freddy meets strange animals,
Panda tames a dangerous dog, Tahiti
starts a promising career, and Vicky
doesn't hesitate to put her life in danger
to get home. And a little clown brings
joy to a house full of sadness.

The Maine Coons

That same evening when Mum picked me up off the pavement and took me home, I discovered curious animals called "Maine Coons". Boy, the house was full of them! But what exactly were they? They had bear paws and raccoon tails and wore silky, long, deluxe coats, almost as if they were going to a ball. And like lynxes, they had whiskers on their pointy ears! At first, I was slightly afraid, but they looked at me so kindly that I thought I would try to charm them a bit. It never hurts, you know. So, I crawled close to the biggest of them – the one the others called "daddy". He was at least ten times bigger than me! Adopting the persona of a cute little kitten, I bent my head down and stuffed it into his thick fur.

And it worked! He leaned over me, licked my fore-head and ears, and kissed me.

"I'm daddy Uddy," he said. "Do you want to be my son?"

Of course, I wanted! I hadn't even known until then that one could have a daddy. My confidence boosted by the addition of an ally, I moved to the next "Maine Coon" – there were seven of them, all standing around me. The next one was a large tabby lady with a long coat that swept the ground. She was probably a princess. I buried myself in her silky fur, and she kissed me and hugged me tight, saying, "There you are, my son. You've come back! I always knew you would".

I didn't understand quite what she was talking about. I only later learned that she was Mummy Tahiti. Her beloved son Maxi had crossed the rainbow bridge a few months ago, and she waited for him to return.

As my approach had been successful with the first two giants, I moved to the other ones and buried my head in their fur. They all kissed and hugged me in turn. I was so happy to be cuddled, given the fear and trauma the yellow monster had put me through!

That's how I got to know Daddy Uddy and Mummy Tahiti and their four daughters – my sisters. Ah, there was also an older gentleman called Uncle Panda. I understood he was the judge of peace.

I no longer cared if they were bears, squirrels, or even lynxes. To me, they were my new family. They loved me, and I loved them at first sight. From that moment on, I became a Maine Coon myself. Okay, a tiny, tiny one, with maybe slightly shorter fur and whisker-free ears.

Later, Mum explained that my new family members were cats, the giant domestic breed. They came from far away, the state of Maine. There, they would use their large, furry paws to walk in deep snow; they would swim in icy rivers to catch fish for breakfast, and when they slept, they had to curl their bushy tails around their faces and shoulders to keep warm. Or they would curl them around their bums to create customised cushions to sit on. One cannot just sit in deep snow. What an adventurous life! I would like to spend time with them in that state of Maine one day. We could make a snowcat and roll around in the snow.

But that life was all before they met Mum. Now, they demand a whole buffet to be served at each meal and fluffy cushions and baskets to be placed throughout the house, preferably right under their noses. So much for the adventure! Ah, everyone aspires to a better standard of living.

I once asked daddy Uddy how he managed to bring his large family across the ocean. Had they just jumped into the big water and, one, two, three, headed for France by swimming across? But he said, no, he hadn't swum over, at least not that he could remember. Harry, our human brother, had gone to fetch him from his breeder's house, and the rest had followed. And a few months before, Harry had come to get Mummy Tahiti.

But the first Maine Coon to arrive at Mum's was Uncle Panda.

Oh, what I was thinking of! I'm telling you all this, and you haven't even met them yet! Come, let's turn the pages and discover their incredible stories!

UDDY

TAHITI

My Funny Uncle Panda

Uncle Panda was Mum's first Maine Coon. He was an extraordinary chap who believed all his dreams would come true. A bit naïve, wasn't he? But that said, many humans are just like him. My Mum is one – she thinks my book will be a success, poor thing! But let's move on.

Interestingly, Panda was right, as what he often wished for would happen! By just believing he could do it, he achieved it. Thus, he became friends with a fierce, dangerous dog; he made a public demonstration he could drive Mum's car; he won a battle with two giant eagle owls who believed he was a snack. And last but not least, he rode a Harley Davidson! And like a king, he had a whole court of squirrels who worshipped him.

However, his most outstanding achievement was getting adopted by Mum when she had no intention of getting another cat.

Here is how it happened.

Choosing His Mum

The first time Panda and Mum met was at a cat show. It was one rainy, gloomy Sunday in February. Mum had just come back from a business trip to Italy. She was depressed. Her beloved cat Chloé had gone over the rainbow bridge just two days before.

Mum had learned of her death while visiting Anagni, a historic town close to Rome. Later, she told us how difficult it was to be hit by this news in such a beautiful place. According to Mum, Anagni is one of central Italy's most picturesque, charming towns. It's perched on a rocky hillside and offers splendid views. When she was visiting, it was Carnival Day. She said the procession on the city's narrow streets was most colourful and hilarious. She felt like a dagger went straight through her heart when she received the news. It was such a contrast with the magic around her! Chloé wasn't very old and was in good health. That day, she had been snacking and playing - and a moment later, she was dead.

No wonder Mum was depressed when she arrived home. There was no cat to greet her, the sky was grey, and it was raining. Fortunately, Dad had a brilliant idea. "Let's go visit a cat exhibition!" he suggested.

As the whole family was enthusiastic, Mum agreed. "But we won't get a cat!" she warned. Of course, it was far too early to bring a new kitty into the house, and everyone felt it.

Everyone? Not quite! A little guy in a remote corner of the exhibition was looking forward to Mum's visit.

"Is she coming yet? I'm fully packed!" he asked his sister as he dropped the last stuffed mouse on the pile in the corner. They were both inside a big cage, next to another one with their parents, two beautiful Maine Coons.

Their breeder, Micheline, had brought all of them to the cat show hoping she could sell the little ones. She wasn't happy, though. It was already late afternoon, the show was closing in a few hours, and virtually no one had shown interest in the two little kittens! It was partly due to the place allocated to her; she was in a dark corner at the end of the big hall.

"*Petits*, you're a hard sell," she said to the kittens.

The little guy replied, "Don't worry, Micheline, I'll be off in a minute!"

The two Maine Coon kittens, a boy and a girl were Panda and Penelope. It was true that there wasn't a crowd around their cage. However, Panda was sure he would not return to Micheline's house! Today was his big day. His Mum would come and collect him and take him to his forever home.

But what was she waiting for? Suddenly he noticed her: she was coming! Panda recognised her from afar.

"Mum, Mum! Meow, here I am! Come and pick me, hurry!"

He quickly gave his paws the last tongue brush, rubbed his eyes, and sat up straight, very close to the bars, to have a better chance of being noticed. There wasn't a mirror close to check his appearance, so he tried to see the reflection in his sister's eyes – was he looking good? But Penelope was already napping.

Never mind, Panda was sure: he'd be out and on his way to his new home one minute more. There was no need for the formalities or other stuff, mainly since he was hungry.

Mum and her family arrived, stopped in front of Panda and Penelope's cage, exchanged a few kind words with the breeder, and – oh, what a disaster! They left.

"Meow, what about me?" shouted Panda. Unfortunately, as he was still tiny, the sound of his little voice was lost in the surrounding chatter. What had just happened was utterly unbelievable. Even his stuffed mice had been deceived.

"Ha," said his sister mockingly, "Your Mum, huh? She hardly noticed you!"

"I thought you were napping?" replied Panda. *Always laughing at me, silly sister*, he thought.

"No worries, she'll come back! I'm sending her a message," he replied. The idea came to him suddenly; he didn't know why. It crackled through his despair like a spark and lit up everything around him. But how to do it when you're just a kitty without a mobile phone? He closed his eyes, concentrated intensely, and wrote in his mind: "Mum, you forgot me! I won't be cross if you come back immediately!" Then he tapped the ground with his tail, and there it was – message sent! No doubt, Mum would be back within minutes.

It wasn't minutes; it was possibly more than an hour before the incredible happened. The exhibition was almost closing; the lights were going out one after the other when suddenly a woman was seen running down the alley, gesturing with her hands towards Micheline.

"Madam, madam! I want one of your little ones! I'll take one of your kittens!" She called from a distance. Micheline, happy and excited, picked Penelope, to Panda's great distress.

"Take the girl," she advised. "They're easier to look after."

Of course, this was not true, but Micheline was anxious to get rid of the girl first. With the Maine Coon breed, the boys grow to a much larger size, and that's why people prefer them. Mum knew which cat she wanted very well but took Penelope in her arms out of politeness.

Panda's sister wouldn't even look at Mum. *Why should I go with her? She's not my Mum*! She thought; she bent her head down and closed her eyes.

"Let me try with the other one," suggested Mum. Now it was Panda's turn to get out of the cage.

Mum took him gently, raised him to the level of her face, and smiled at him. *Yes*, she thought *this was the kitten I wanted,* not knowing yet that Panda wasn't a kitten -he was a little boy. Panda smiled back (of course, he did) gave her three butterfly kisses - one on her nose and one on each of her cheeks - and said, "Meow!" to confirm the deal. It was his signature at the bottom of the love contract-a lifetime one, with an extended warranty through eternity.

But what exactly had happened? Why had Mum suddenly decided to come back when she had already returned home and had her afternoon tea? No one knows – certainly not me. One very wise cat told me once that it may have been teleph. . ., "telepathy" (I think), or at least something similar.

Train Journey

Unlike me, Panda loved travelling. He was happy as long as it moved, whether it was a car or a train. However, his train journey always started with a bit of annoyance. Mum would arrive with Panda at the railway station and ask for the tickets at the counter. "For myself and my cat," she would say.

Without replying, the cashier would issue two tickets. Cashiers in France never say "Bonjour" or "Yes, madame" or any other little words that customers may appreciate. They're way above that. They're not going to stoop to being courteous to customers, are they? Besides, nobody calls them customers – they're just annoying travellers, and the French railway world would be so beautiful without them!

Mum would then check the tickets and inevitably notice the allocation on Panda's one. It would say "little dog"!

"But, monsieur," she would object, "he's not a dog; he's a cat!"

"It's the same thing," the cashier would reply, shouting. When they need to answer, cashiers at railway stations shout. We don't know why they do it. Is this to intimidate customers and prevent them from asking further questions? Or maybe to demonstrate their high rank on the railway? Anyway, I think it's time cats take over railway station counters – at least they know what good manners are!

Unhappy, Mum would go to look for her train, mumbling something about people who need glasses. She never dared show Panda his ticket. He would have been most put out! If only the words had been "big dog"!

Once on the train, Mum would take Panda out of his carrier and install him next to her. Thus, he could watch all the passengers passing by, and if they looked at him, he would call out to them: "Meow! How are you today?"

Most of them would stop for a few seconds to compliment him on his beauty. Still, if someone passed without saying anything or smiling, Panda would become very offended. "What's wrong with this one? Why doesn't he say I'm beautiful?"

Mum usually went to the bar car for a coffee break, as the journey was rather long. She would take Panda in her arms and walk through the carriages. Mum would get a coffee and Panda, the cream served on a little saucer. They settled down next to a window to admire the scenery and enjoy the break. While Mum would sip her coffee, Panda would wash down the cream.

Although he was free during the whole journey, it never occurred to Panda to leave Mum for a second and go for a walk on the train by himself.

Driving a Car

Have you ever seen a cat driving a car? Not that our Panda could do it, but he publicly demonstrated his ability to operate it if it was ever needed. Mum told us this story.

Back then, Panda was Mum's sole cat, and whenever the family had to travel, he would go with them, be it on a train, on a plane, or by car.

Cars were his passion, as were motorbikes. Quite normal for a little boy. Just as in the train, Panda also travelled freely in the car. He would sit on the back seat or the rear plate, looking at the landscape and marvelling at the passing motorbikes. As soon as a big motorbike passed the car, Panda would jump from the seat, stomp, meow, and scratch the window. "Mum, meow," he would shout, "did you see that one? It was so beautiful! Say, Mum, can I have one of those for my birthday?"

"Of course, you can, darling," Mum would say to ensure some quiet time during the drive.

Usually, Mum would do the driving and Dad the criticising. The responsibilities in a household must be shared fairly. Panda would observe. Driving, he thought, was not so difficult. Besides, Mum made all kinds of mistakes – you only had to listen to Dad! He could carry on a bit. "You drive too fast!" "Don't overtake; there's no room!" "Careful! What are you doing now?" "Speed up, overtake the truck. What are you waiting for?" And so on. Panda quickly concluded that Mum was a lousy driver. But he, Panda, would undoubtedly be able to do much better.

So, one day, when the car had stopped at a gas station and Mum and Dad went for a coffee break, he decided to try his hand at the wheel. He moved across from the back to the driver's seat. Looking very serious, sitting upright on his bum, he put his paws on the steering wheel and looked straight ahead. You need to keep an eye on the road when you drive. He started to move his paws like he had seen Mum move her hands. Occasionally, he pressed the horn, located in the centre of the steering wheel, by jumping on it with the forepart of his body. He needed to warn people - the car would move forward at any time. Recognising the sound of their horn, Mum and Dad came running out of the coffee shop. They saw a crowd surrounding their car, so they had to make their way through it to discover what was going on.

And there he was: their beloved kitty behind the wheel with a severe look on his face, pretending to drive and looking like he would be starting the car any minute.

"Look, a cat is driving!" shouted the crowd; people pulled out their mobile phones to capture the scene.

Regrettably, Panda was obliged to leave the steering wheel to Mum for the rest of the journey. But at least he had proved that he could drive. If Dad weren't happy with Mum, he would know who to turn to!

The Cat Killer Dog

The neighbour at our seaside home had a big dog. Mum said it was a Labrador. This neighbour was always bragging to Mum: "My dog is a cat killer. No cat dares enter our garden. If the dog sees it, he chases it immediately. And, if he wanted to, he could kill it!"

Mum didn't believe him. This dog was massive, fat, and unlikely to catch a cat.

However, she remained alert and carefully protected the fence between the two homes. "Don't go to the other side, Panda," she'd say. "Don't even put a paw under the fence – the dog on the other side is not a nice dog."

Panda, too, didn't believe it. Not a friendly dog? Quite impossible! All dogs are nice. You have to know how to talk to them; Mum was telling nonsense. Besides, he had a plan.

One sunny morning close to noon, Mum suddenly noticed Panda heading towards the neighbour's house. He was slowly strolling along the narrow railing. She considered shouting, but Panda was already on the boundary between the two properties. If frightened, he might fall – possibly onto the neighbour's side. Mum's heart stopped beating for a few seconds. The huge dog on the other side was looking at Panda, patiently awaiting his visit.

Panda crossed, jumped down next to the dog very calmly, and gave him a light nose touch.

I imagine he said something like, "Hello, neighbour! Nice to finally meet you! How are you today?"

The dog opened his colossal mouth and stuck out his tongue. Mum's blood ran cold. Was he going to swallow the cat? Although Panda was a big Maine Coon, it was still possible.

But no! He engulfed Panda's entire head in a long, slow kiss with his enormous tongue. Well, I guessed it was hot and sticky! Then they both sat down to have a little chat.

Unfortunately, Panda had to leave – Mum was tempting him with roast chicken on the other side of the fence. That day, the most significant piece of the chicken was for the dog – to thank him for the warm welcome. Panda himself helped push it under the fence.

After that event, the dog's owner got embarrassed and stopped boasting about his dog being a cat killer. Especially since the dog and the cat had become best friends.

Squirrels, Eagle-Owls, and the Escape

There are many other stories about my Uncle Panda. For example, how he spied on the squirrels at the end of every afternoon and ran to the kitchen, trembling with excitement, to alert Mum: it was feeding time! Then they both came out with bags of nuts to treat the Panda's friends.

Or how he chased away two giant eagle-owls who came to visit one night believing that this kitty would make a good snack. Or again, how he decided to go around the world one day and left home. After a day and a night out, he returned with his claws worn a bit and his paws dirty. No one knows where he went or what he did. He only said, "The world tour wasn't worth it," and sat down to gobble two dinners in a row.

Birthday Treat

Panda's greatest passion was motorbikes. The bigger they were, the more ecstatic he was about them. Every time he heard the roar of a big motorcycle engine, he'd get incredibly excited. He'd jump up and down, meow and call Mum.

One day, a contractor who was doing some work on our house arrived with his Harley Davidson. Panda was thrilled. The bike was beautiful; it was brand new, shiny and sparkling. My Uncle kept circling it as it was standing in the drive alley.

The contractor asked Mum: "What's going on with that cat? Does he like motorbikes?"

"Yes," replied Mum. "He'd like to go for a ride."

"A ride?" repeated the amused entrepreneur. "Why not? Let's go!" With that, he picked Panda up and installed him in the saddlebag of the luggage rack.

"Come on, big guy, but take care. Hold on tight!" he advised before starting the bike. Had you thought Panda would have jumped down to save himself? I would! But instead, he looked pleased. His tail was waving, his face shone with happiness, his paws trampled the saddlebag, and he purred loudly. Imagine, the biggest dream of his life was coming true!

The contractor took three very slow laps around the garden with the cat at his back.

"You see," Mum said to Panda after thanking the obedient man, "you got your bike ride right on your birthday! What a beautiful present!" Indeed, it was November 9, his birthday.

Not long after that, he went to another neighbour's garden to see if there were any new dogs to charm or some squirrels in need of nuts. But he always came back, or someone would bring him home. For, you know, my uncle was famous in our neighbourhood. He walked through life with big, trusting eyes believing the world was full of friendly creatures who all adored him and wanted to do him good. And somehow, he was right; everyone loved him, and he loved everyone, be they people or animals. I often saw him talking kindly to birds and the mice inside the hedge.

He was a happy kitty and had a wonderful, long life.

PANDA

The Kitty Who Wouldn't Be Left Alone

Mum's second Maine Coon cat was called Tahiti. Actually, at first, she lived with my human brother, Harry. He had gone to fetch her from her breeder's house when he moved into his new flat.

It was a lovely flat with a balcony for a cat to step out, hiss at its peers, call the birds, and watch hedges from afar. But, oh boy, there was no cat. Just unthinkable! Imagine: you come home, tired after a long day of work. You open the door, and there is no one to jump around you and stop you from taking off your coat and shoes. No one to demand to know your whereabouts: "Where have you been? What have you brought for me?" There is no one to want a multitude of things from you immediately – litter box cleaning, a meal to be served, and cuddles to be shared. So many needs that must be taken care of all at once! It makes your head spin, and you don't know where to start.

How can anyone live without a cat and miss such a thrill?

Urgent action was needed. One early Sunday afternoon, Harry jumped in his car and set off to Micheline's little breeding farm. Micheline was the lady from the cat show where Mum found her first Maine Coon, my uncle Panda.

On the way, he thought about which cat he would choose - preferably a male, as they get bigger. Maybe a ginger one? Harry liked ginger cats.

But in Micheline's house was a tiny kitten named Tahiti who had quite different plans. She knew her new daddy would come that Sunday, so she woke up very early, washed her beautiful coat three times, and cleaned her eyes five times. (She only briefly slipped her paws behind her ears because she didn't like washing them.) Once she had finished grooming, she went to admire herself in the large mirror in Micheline's room.

"Mirror, mirror on the wall, who is the prettiest of them all?" she asked but did not wait for an answer.

What was the point? She was, of course! No one would dare dispute it; let them try – she would show them! She went to the front door, jumped on a stool and settled comfortably. Who knew when this young man would arrive? He may have been delayed by traffic or the weather; Tahiti hadn't listened to that morning's weather forecast.

Curious and intrigued, her two sisters came running up. "Tahiti, what are you doing here? Why don't you come and play? Who are you waiting for? Can we wait with you?"

Oh, those sisters. Always so intrusive! Tahiti didn't even reply. Pffft, who did they think they were, asking all those questions? They were just cats, while she, ha, was a cat with a dad. Well, almost. But she had to wait quite some time; the road from Paris to the Loire Valley is long. When finally, a car stopped in front of Micheline's little house, she jumped up and shouted: "It's him! He's arrived! He's here!"

Her sisters rushed to the door to help with the welcome: "He's here, he's here! Meow, meow!"

Tahiti hissed at them: "Go away! He came to fetch me, not you!" And although she was the smallest of the three, she added: "Out of my sight, you little copycats!"

When Harry stepped inside the house, she looked at him, and her heart started beating fast. "Oh, he's just as I imagined! So tall and so handsome!" she exclaimed. She would have gladly jumped in his arms right away, but she remembered what her grandmother had always said: "Girls should not be too eager." So, she followed him until he sat on the sofa at Micheline's invitation. Ah, that was the green light! She jumped on his lap - she had to charm him immediately. She would not let him come to his senses and look at the other kittens – possibly at the ginger cat he had dreamt of. Granted, the ginger cat didn't even live in this house but better to be safe than sorry.

Once on Harry's lap, the kitten started to purr louder than a plane taking off, rubbed her head against her new dad's hands, and looked at him with devotion and love. Her sisters also wanted to spend time on the young man's lap. It seemed like a fun game. He was giving Tahiti so many cuddles; there would undoubtedly be some for them, wouldn't they? There were, but oh dear, this Tahiti wouldn't let them approach! Each time they got close, she would slap them and hiss furiously: "Get your paws off! Don't you dare touch my daddy!"

Not even a joint attempt at crawling along Harry's legs helped. Their trick was discovered and rewarded by Tahiti's furious hissing and smacking.

"Nobody will steal my daddy away!" declared Tahiti and put on the most murderous look she was capable of. (Between you and me, it wasn't much – it wouldn't have scared anyone, not even a mouse.)

After a short while, it became clear to all present, cats and humans, that Harry had no choice. Had he wanted to get a ginger boy? Well, he'd be going away with a tabby girl. So, he signed a few papers and settled the kitty into a carrier. Tahiti said goodbye to her sisters, promising that she'd come to visit soon. Then they left. We don't know which of them was more delighted.

They reached Mum's home late that afternoon to make the necessary introductions. Uncle Panda didn't show any eagerness or joy to meet his half-sister (they had the same Maman). He looked at her with an air of "What are you doing here? Why did you come?" then turned to the wall and pretended to be asleep.

Mum, on the other hand, was enchanted. She loved the kitty at first sight. As for Tahiti, she had decided that Panda was "a boring grumpy oldie" and that

Mum was "Panda's Mum", hence totally uninteresting (except for the treats she kept offering). Besides, Tahiti never liked girls.

Then, tired after a day of so many emotions, they went to Harry's flat, a place that should be her forever home.

But it wasn't going to be. As soon as the next day, things started to go wrong.

After sharing breakfast, her dad announced, "I'm going to the office now. I'll be back at the end of the day."

Naturally, she was going too, so she licked her beautiful coat and cleaned her eyes with her paws. It was essential to make a good impression on her first day. But oh, surprise! Dad put on his shoes and jacket, grabbed his bag, and gave her a quick kiss on the head.

"See you tonight. I'm already late," he said. And he left!

At first, the surprise took her breath away. How come her dad dared to leave her alone? It just cannot be! She started calling loudly: "Dad, you forgot something! You forgot Tahiti!" She listened, hoping that she would hear his steps - he would come back to fetch her! But he didn't.

That was a betrayal! She would not have chosen him for a dad if she had known! What could she do now? She noticed a security camera pointing at the door. Ah, this was interesting! Dad would definitely check on her while at work (all dads check on their kids). So, she waited a bit, leaving him time to reach his office and chat at the coffee machine – a must in French offices. Then the play began. The scene was written by herself, and she was in the starring role. The drama's title was: *The Cat Who Wouldn't Be Left Alone*. Obviously.

She scratched the door and cried. She meowed endlessly. She repeatedly sat close to the camera, looking straight into it with her most depressing look. She stretched out on the carpet and pretended she wasn't feeling well. After a while, she started walking in circles, meowing so desperately that even a stone would pity her. And although she was getting hungry, she never went near her bowl of biscuits or the water – she was so poorly and far too desperate to eat (ha). She meowed and meowed all day long.

Who could not believe such a good actor? Her dad, worried, rushed home from the office earlier than usual.

"Something is wrong with Tahiti," he said to Mum. "I think she's seriously ill."

But once her dad was home, Tahiti became a happy little kitten again, full of life and mischief. She played with her dad for hours; they shared dinner and bed – and breakfast the following day. No doubt, this time, her dad would take her with him! But oh surprise, he left alone! He even seemed happy.

"All is fine," he said to Mum. "It was just her first day alone. She'll get used to the flat."

But she didn't. She kept complaining so loudly that even the neighbours were beginning to wonder what was happening. Harry decided to call Micheline for advice.

"Oh, I forgot to tell you! This kitty cannot be left alone," said the breeder. Well, it was about time Harry learned that!

"Let's take her to the office," suggested Mum. And so it was done, much to Tahiti's satisfaction.

At that time, Mum and Harry worked together in Mum's small company and drove to the office each morning. And the little tabby cat became part of the journey from the following Monday.

* * *

In the Office (Told by Tahiti Herself)

Once we got to the office, they opened the carrier, and I stepped out. Pffft, it wasn't as I had imagined it. It didn't look like the Oval Office or the *president's* office at the Elysée palace! However, it was a vast open space with plenty of opportunities to sprint around. I decided I liked it.

But holy cow, what a mess! It was about time I came on board. All the desks were cluttered with piles of documents and files. And those office plants! They looked like nothing; they had no decent shape. I decided to start with those two tasks before the staff arrived. First, I jumped on one desk after another, pushing the papers and files onto the carpet to make the place clean. Once the desks were ready, the employees could start their shifts. Next, I went to the plants. They desperately needed proper restyling. Some were huge, but I wasn't put off. I bravely climbed up them and gave them each a makeover; I snatched the leaves and threw them down or chewed them into more pleasing shapes.

When the staff arrived, they gave me an appropriately welcoming reception. I was expecting a big party with champagne and a red carpet. But it seemed they preferred a blue rug and coffee in this office – they drank it all day long. So much that I wondered what this company was all about. Were they a coffee testing company? I didn't mind, as long as they shared the cream with me.

As I discovered over the next few days, there was no shortage of work for me. So many tasks were just perfectly tailored for a cat. For example, printing. Papers flew out of that big machine that you, Freddy, would undoubtedly have mistaken for the yellow monster. Of course, they all needed my approval before being sent to customers. So I had to put my scratch on each of them. Wasn't I the head of the office?!

They also needed my help to answer the phone. The calls were so numerous in this office, it never stopped! I had to jump from one desk to the other and meow in all known languages. It's a good thing I'm a multilingual cat. You see, it was an international company. Soon, clients from all around the world enjoyed discussing unit prices and ship-ment costs with me. They even started refusing to talk to Mum, the boss! And I do not want to get anyone into trouble, but I had to correct each email before it was sent out! You know, those geek employees tended to forget everything about spelling. I can't count how many times I had to add a whole series of 'n' and 'o" and 'x' to their messages. Nobody is better at spelling than a cat, as you may know.

Oh, and how much I enjoyed lunchtime. The office building was on a pedestrian street, with plenty of roast chicken shops. The staff would go out to buy food, and when they got back, we would all sit down in their tiny kitchen and share. I mean, they shared, and I ate. What a feast we had each day!

Over a few days, I trained them to ask for 'very crispy roast chicken for the cat' down at the shops. It was very wise as it helped me become the pedestrian street celebrity. . .

One of the staff members, usually David, the webmaster, would place my order: "Please may I have this beautiful crispy piece? The cat will love it."

"What cat?" the shopkeeper would ask.

"We have a little kitten in the office."

"Oh, unbelievable! Can we come up and see it?"

And they did come, one after another. I always let the visitors cuddle me and take pictures to please my team. Some arrived with a present for me, and they deserved my head rubs and nose kisses. They loved it! I became so popular in the area that I wondered why they didn't rename the street "Tahiti's Street"? Or even the city "Tahiti's City". It would have been the least they could do, wouldn't it?

As my career was taking off, my dad announced it was holiday time, and I had to go with Panda and Mum to the seaside. He would be touring Europe. I wasn't enchanted; I would gladly have gone with him. I hoped, however, to see him again in September, especially since I didn't like the place Mum took me on holiday.

But I'll let Mum tell this bit since she is the one to blame for what happened.

TAHITI

Holiday

It was the first time I had taken Tahiti to our seaside home – she had been with us for three months. We arrived late, and she didn't have time to explore the place. It was only in the morning that I took the cats outside onto the terrace. It had rained all night, and the floor was slippery. I walked towards the west side, where we had our little dining area overlooking the sea to enjoy breakfast together. They walked ahead of me. Panda, with the assurance of a home-owner, proud and happy to show the premises to his half-sister, and Tahiti trotting slowly behind him, careful and curious at the same time. Good sign, I thought; at least she won't dare climb the railing. But I had barely formed the thought when she took off in one go, landed on the round table, which was all soggy with rain, and slipped and slipped and disap-peared – straight over the railing! All I heard was the sound of her tiny body as it hit the ground. We were very high on the first floor, and below the terrace, the ground was hard and dry with no vegetation to break her fall. She must have hurt herself badly because the sound of her fall was so loud that it scared me. I leaned over the barrier. She was nowhere to be seen – she had disappeared in a split second.

Panda didn't look; much wiser than I, he quickly ran to the front door, meowing. He wanted to go out and search for her. He was right; it was urgent that we, or rather I, go outside and find her. A small pine forest surrounded the house; did she run into it? How could I see her there? It was a dark place, with bushes and high pine trees. Numerous animals strolled at night: rabbits, owls and even foxes. Everything would be unfamiliar to her. When we arrived the previous night, we parked in the garage and went upstairs straightaway without stepping outside. The poor kitty surely wouldn't know where she was.

I put my dressing gown on over my pyjamas and, still in slippers, ran downstairs. The gardens around the building were huge and descended into terraces towards the sea. Of course, it was beautiful but not meant for one to take a stroll. Narrow paths ran between the bushes; the undergrowth blocked the way, and "decorative" rocks were everywhere. Everything was soggy as it rained all night, and it was hard to progress in slippers. I looked around and called her name. "Tahiti! Tahiti!" I looked under every bush, inspected every hedge and searched inside the flower beds. I found some snails, but that was all. Here and there, among the rocks and low vegetation, tall pine trees rose to the sky. I looked up – maybe she had climbed up one of them?

And that was where I saw them: all the people on their balconies in the opposite building, silently watching me. It was incredible. There were tens and tens of them leaning over and looking at me. Obviously, without knowing it, I had become an attraction. I must have looked a sight with my hair down, in my pyjamas, dressing gown, and slippers. I was calling Tahiti's name. That had probably also created the impression that I was extremely confused; we weren't on the Tahiti archipelago here; we were in Brittany! They visibly had no intention of asking me what or who I was looking for, let alone offering assistance.

Astonished but not discouraged, I kept searching. I don't know how long I stayed in the gardens. It was still early, the air was chilly, and my slippers were wet. I decided to go inside and get a cup of warm coffee before resuming my search. Maybe I could even spot the kitty from the terrace. . .

Then, just before entering the building, I stopped. Let's imagine I'm a cat who had just fallen from the balcony, hurt herself a bit, and discovered that everything around was strange, unknown. What would I do? Would I run down into the gardens or the forest, even more intimidating? Certainly not. I would have been too scared. So, where would I have gone?

I looked around the spot where she must have landed. There were a few little bushes, but most were too small to be used as hiding places, except for one. A little bit to the side stood a colossal hydrangea bush. I pulled the stems apart – they were tall and dense, and it was very dark in the centre of the plant. I looked inside, trying to differentiate the ground from the dead leaves and spot something that would look like fur. Tabby kitties and dead leaves have something in common; their colours are alike. I couldn't see anything and wanted to walk away. But first, I called her name one more time. "Tahiti!"

"Meow," replied the lump of soil and leaves in the centre of the plant. It was a tiny meow, barely audible. I dug up the little darling, hugged her small body full of soil and took her into the house. Panda was so happy! He danced around her, meowed and wanted to lick her head. But I took her straight to the bathroom, under the shower. She liked it! I bet she was freezing, as I was.

The remainder of our holiday went smoothly. Tahiti didn't show any further interest in going outside. She preferred chasing spiders and dragonflies around the terrace when she wasn't trying to imitate Spiderman. She loved climbing walls, and her aim was to get as high as possible before sliding down.

* * *

Big Changes Ahead

Freddy here; I'm back! Those two ladies hijacked my story, and they kept talking to my readers! Incredible; who is the author here?! They never let me get a word in. I showed them off, but now I'm here to tell you what happened the following autumn.

Although Tahiti expected to resume her office career, Harry and Mum decided it wasn't the best idea.

"I'll get her a brother so that she won't be bored when she's alone in the flat," declared Harry and set off again for Micheline's breeding farm.

That's how a tiny little black and white guy arrived at Mum's home – Uddy, the third Maine Coon. And soon, he was to become "Daddy Uddy". With his arrival, essential changes were ahead for Mum and her cats, as you'll discover in the following few stories.

My Daddy's Cat Big Adventure

When my Daddy Uddy was a kitten, his breeder didn't like him. She called him "ugly duckling" and decided to get rid of him as soon as a buyer showed up on the doorstep. Luckily that buyer happened to be my human brother Harry.

But before starting a happy life in his forever home, Uddy had to go through some dreadful events. Here is the story he told me:

Planning an Escape

When I was little, my breeder locked me into a dark room with just a plate of cat biscuits and water. It's terrible being locked in a dark room, you know Freddy, I hated it. Some people think that we cats can see in the dark, but we can't; we need a bit of light coming from somewhere to make something out of it. From the first hour in that dark room, I dreamt about escaping. I wondered, there must be a place where my breeder couldn't find me. I saw a bright disc high above, climbing behind the heavy drapery on the window, at night. I thought, oh, that's the place I need to go! They certainly don't have dark rooms up there, do they? It looks so wonderfully bright!

So, on the second day of my confinement, I decided to try my luck. I stood behind the door when the breeder entered with fresh water, and just before she left, I sneaked out. I skimmed the walls and found the kitchen – it was so beautiful and bright inside. A large beam of light was falling through the open window. I thought that was the path to freedom. Someone from that bright disc might send it down for me to climb onto it. I only needed to jump into that brightness, and it would embrace me and lift me into the sky.

But before that, I wanted to get some food. The way up might take a bit long. I'd had no time to swallow any biscuits before escaping. Here in the kitchen, the air was full of delightful smells. I jumped on the table and started to look around for some good food, something easy to take with me. That's when I heard the heavy footsteps of the breeder approaching.

Quick! I had to get out of this place! She mustn't catch me; I didn't want to be shut up again. I closed my eyes and jumped as high and far as possible, directly into the light beam, hoping it would carry me to the sky.

But it didn't, Freddy. First, I heard the birds singing. Then I heard bees buzzing. A tiny voice asked, "Do you want to play with me?" And I finally dared open my eyes.

I was somewhere outside, hidden inside the tall grass. A blue butterfly spun around my head, tickled my nose, and laughed. Oh, this looked so much better than the dark room! I thought that I had already landed on that shiny disc. But I quickly realised I was just in the garden and far too close to the kitchen. So I whispered, "Oh, thank you, that's so kind of you, but I'm going to the bright disc."

"To where?" asked the surprised butterfly.

"To the bright thing in the sky," I explained and ran forward through the tall grass. I was frightened the breeder would come after me, grab me by the scruff of my neck, and carry me into that dark room again. And who knows if she wouldn't also lock me in the carrier as she'd done once before?

"Cats should be punished like children," she explained to our Mum a month later when they met. "They have to learn to obey. We shouldn't let them get into bad habits."

Mum smiled politely, but she was horrified. She started to think about how she could have all the cats taken away from this breeding farm and spare them any further punishment. But, of course, there was no easy way to do this. The breeder had many cats, and some weren't even up for sale.

Freddy, you may ask what I did to deserve the punishment, at least in the eyes of my breeder. Well, Freddy, I only asked for cuddles. You see, she was always cuddling Uranus, my brother. Not that I'm a jealous chap, you know. However, I was always pushed away when I asked for something, and would it be treats, a toy, or a hug. Uranus was the family darling – he got the tastiest food, new catnip toys that smelled so good, and lots of kisses and cuddles every day. I never got them, and I would have been so grateful for even a stroke or two! On the day she had locked me in the dark room, it was because I knocked over a vase. Accidentally, of course; besides, it was her fault - she had pushed me away when I wanted to climb onto her lap. You talk about a loss! That vase was so depressingly ugly; it was about time someone took care of it. She should have thanked me, not punished me! No, Freddy, I knew my actual fault lay elsewhere. I had the silly idea of coming into the world as a black and white kitty. On seeing me, the breeder had exclaimed, "What! A black and white cat in my breeding? I've only had beautiful tabbies for decades! I don't want him! I'll sell him to the first buyer that comes in!"

So, she left me all alone, hardly ever took care of me, and, above all, never cuddled me. On top of this, my Mummy cat Steffi also preferred my brother as he was almost her clone. I was not the right colour for this household, you see. They called me 'the ugly duckling'. Imagine, Freddy! I'm first and foremost not a duck! And I'm not ugly, am I? No one wanted to play with me in that house. I was so miserable!

Being punished made me realise that asking humans for hugs can be dangerous. Even nowadays, I never go to Mum to cuddle like the rest of you, Freddy.

But back then, in the tall grass, I forgot all; nothing mattered anymore. I was just happily running away; I couldn't stop singing to myself out of joy. My purring echoed through the tall grass to the amazement of the bumblebees, who probably wondered who this four-legged competitor was.

Finding New Friends

Soon, I reached the end of the garden. Oh, but what was this on the other side of the fence? Some kind of a giant white animal in the meadow! How strange, it seemed to be eating grass. Was the grass so tasty on the other side? Maybe I should try some, I thought. But how to get over the fence? I started to climb, and you know what, it was even easier than climbing the couch or the bookshelf! And in addition, nobody was shouting at me.

Once on the other side, I cried, "Hello, mister!" It's better to treat someone deferentially when you see such an enormous being. "May I come closer?"

"Hey, there's a little kitten!" whinnied the animal, galloping towards me. Once he reached me, he bent his enormous head down and smelled me with his big nostrils. They were so warm and soft! It felt like sweet kisses.

"Ooh, ooh! That's so kind!" I said. "Thank you, mister. What's your name, sir?"

"I'm Pegasus, the horse. And who are you, sonny?"

"I'm Uddy", I replied, because, you know, like all smart kids, I knew my name, my address, and my telephone number. What? You don't believe me, Freddy? Well, maybe not the telephone number. . .

"*Enchanté*, Uddy!" You see, this horse was a tiny bit snob. He explained later that being on a farm doesn't mean you can't feel like an aristocrat, a racehorse.

"Do you want to be my friend?" he asked, and I jumped for joy. Friend? But of course, yes! What a wonderful invitation! What a welcome! I'd never had a friend before!

Of course, we became true mates instantly. We played catch-me-if-you-can all day long. We also tried hide-and-seek, but my new friend was too big to hide in the grass, even when he lay down, and I was too small, so he battled to find me.

When the sun started to set and the evening began to creep in, my friend suggested I go home: "Sonny, you should go home now and come again tomorrow to play some more."

Home? I started to shiver. The breeder would undoubtedly be very angry with me for having escaped. I feared the worst: I feared being shut in that dark room again and maybe even being locked in the carrier and not being given any cat biscuits! And I was so hungry! I didn't want to go back. *That house isn't my home anymore*, I thought.

My clear-sighted friend immediately detected a slight problem.

"You may prefer to come to the stable with me? We'll find some good milk for you. Betty, the sheep, had a lamb a few days ago, and Marguerite, the cow, had a calf last night. There is plenty of milk. They will love sharing it with you, I'm sure!"

And, Freddy, that's how I became a member of this small but unique animal community. All these different species sheltered together in the ramshackle little stable on the farm – you see, they were relatively poor.

The tiny community welcomed me with the most extraordinary delight: Marguerite the cow licked my head with her enormous tongue (hmm, it was a bit rough), Betty the sheep offered head bumps, and Benedict the piglet asked if I knew how to count. When he learned I didn't, he offered to teach me. The calf and the lamb wanted to show me a new game, but Pegasus asked them to leave me alone – it was time for dinner. A large milk container was already waiting for us - the farmer had delivered it before I'd arrived. And Benedict pushed under my nose some good chicken soup, the leftover from his dinner. Boy! I don't know if it was because I was so hungry, but I believe it was my best dinner ever! A far cry from the biscuits and water in that dark room!

Farm Life and the Geese Network

That first night, to avoid making anyone jealous, I divided my time between them. I started by sleeping with Pegasus, moved to the calf, then to Betty and the little lamb, before finishing my night by cuddling up to Benedict.

Pegasus woke me early. He said we needed to go out before the farmer arrived to clean the stable. If he found me, he would likely take me back to my breeder, and this nobody wanted to happen.

So, we ran out and had another day of fun in the meadow. It was all play and jumping around until the afternoon when we lay down in the shade of an old chestnut tree. It was time for a nap. Pegasus then told me the story of his ancestor, also named Pegasus, who was a winged horse. At the end of his life, he became one of the brightest stars.

"I'll show it to you one night," he promised. I told him about my dream of going up to that bright disc, the one you can see in the night sky, and I assured him to visit his ancestor once I was up there. You see, Freddy, my dream had not left me.

Here, I had to interrupt Daddy Uddy. I had become frightened. "Hey, Daddy, surely by now you don't still dream of going to the bright disc, do you? If you ever go away, Daddy dear, my heart would split in two and stop beating altogether. You must never leave without me! Never! Do you hear me?"

Daddy Uddy smiled but didn't reply. This left me a bit worried, but I wanted to hear more about his life on the farm, so I asked him to resume.

The calf and the lamb arrived to join us in the late afternoon; they were allowed to run out and stretch their legs for a bit. Ha, this was a lot of fun! While Pegasus grazed on some more tasty weeds, we, the toddlers, ran around, tried all sorts of clumsy acro-batics, chased each other, and laughed and laughed. Back in the stable, we shared milk and soup and curled up, all three of us together, for a bit of cuddling before falling asleep. What an extraordinary change from the dark room in the breeder's house!

The only one who wasn't happy was Benedict. He wanted to teach me many things, like counting up to 10 and big and small letters, but I had no time! I was too busy. I had so many games to play with my friends! So many jumps to jump and so many races to run! The only thing I wanted to learn from Benedict was how to get to that shiny disc in the sky. But he explained that it was called the moon, and it wasn't worth it.

"You see,' he said, "it's a has-been trick. It's been done before. What you need, Uddy is to go to Mars. But hurry up before that human gets ahead of you, that Mewlon Husk," he advised. Benedict was a kind of visionary piglet.

"Who's that?" I asked and promptly fell asleep, too tired to listen any longer. Besides, why bother? Life was so beautiful on the farm with my friends.

And it could have gone on like that for days and days if it weren't for the geese. Those ladies had a broadcasting network, one of those modern channels where the same report is broadcast daily. And repeated hour after hour and also the next day if you didn't get it the first 100 times. DG News was called – Dumb Goosish News. So, when they noticed my presence, they started shouting. . . err . . . broadcasting to the yard, "Alert, alert a meow in the stable. Big danger! Alert! Black and white alien!"

At first, the farmer paid no attention, mainly since the ducks, who liked me very much, shouted in response, "Fake news! Fake news!"

But, as you would expect with all this social networking, the news spread like wildfire. The birds on the trees around the farm started tweeting: "Emergency call! Giant black and white meow beast there, in the stable! Run for life!"

The squirrels on the old chestnut tree looked at each other and whispered, "Extreme danger! A meow, a big black and white one!"

And instead of calling people to mass – as they should have since it was a Sunday morning – the silly church bells Tik-Tok-ed, "Make flight, run away! Alien, alien in the stable! It's even said he's black and white!"

The farmer started to think there could be something behind this noise. It couldn't be on so many social networks without being authentic, could it? So, early that Sunday morning, he entered the stable while we were all still asleep.

Ah, dear Freddy, it was the end of my freedom! I had to say goodbye to my friends with tears in my eyes. But I promised to revisit them. One day, we will go together, Freddy. It will have to be soon; all this happened almost 19 years ago!

I feared the worst when the farmer rang the doorbell at my breeder's house, holding me in his arms. But believe it or not, it was my lucky day! That same afternoon, our human brother Harry was due to come to look at the kittens. He wanted to get another kitten to keep Tahiti company. Our readers know from one of your previous stories, Freddy, that she couldn't be left alone.

When the breeder saw me in the farmer's arms, she immediately thought she had better get rid of me that same day; I was a 'difficult cat'. So, the deal was done as soon as Harry arrived. To the breeder's great surprise, Harry liked me at first sight.

That same afternoon, I met uncle Panda and Tahiti and, above all, our Mum! A wonderful life was about to begin for me.

I must admit that my relationship with Tahiti didn't start out well. I don't know if this girl thought I was her new toy or what, but she kept chasing me around! Luckily, uncle Panda always stepped in the middle to protect me, which stopped her attacks. That problem quickly disappeared; the girl fell in love with me, as I had expected. We became friends and even got married in secret. Soon, Tahiti became Mummy Tahiti, and the house was full of kittens. But more about that in the following story.

Just one word about my breeder, the woman who believed I was ugly. As soon as I grew up a little, Mum sent her my photo. Ah, that was a surprise for her! She immediately called Mum and asked to come to visit "to discuss things". She wanted to repurchase me, offered to pay any price, whatever Mum wanted. When Mum declined the offer, she begged her to 'lend' me for a cat show or two. Suddenly, my breeder wanted to show me to the whole world, to show everyone what a beautiful, handsome Maine Coon her breeding farm had produced. She said I would have won all the competitions, anywhere.

The Biggest Mistake? Well done!

Over the years, the breeder would often come to our house to admire me and always begged Mum to give me back. This woman who had mistreated me when I was a kitten and had called me an ugly duckling had realised her mistake. "The biggest mistake in my whole Maine Coon breeding career," she used to say.

I always turn my back on her whenever she comes to visit, and I walk away. I am happy to be here with you all, glad to be the 'daddy cat' of such a large and beautiful family. I love you all, Freddy.

* * *

When my Dad stopped talking, I thought of the many things that hadn't yet been told about him. How he welcomed me when Mum brought me home for the first time, how he fought with a giant fox to save me, how he freed a little bird that I had brought home for lunch and taught me that birds are not food, and so many things.

My marvellous, wonderful Dad. I think I'll need to write another story about him pretty soon as I love him just too much.

UDDY

Miracle Kittens

When Harry brought Uddy from the breeder to his flat and introduced him to Tahiti, he was convinced she would be so happy! Just imagine, a cute "brother" with whom to play, have fun, share treats and plot adventures! Ah, but the tabby kitty did not see it that way.

"Pffft, go home, little toad!" she hissed, growling at him as soon as he stepped out of the carrier. He even got a big paw-blow on the head as a welcome present! Was he thinking of staying for dinner? Or maybe even sharing the bed and snuggling next to her daddy? No way! She hadn't invited him, so she had to stop things before they started. And Tahiti knew how to anticipate.

Before her Daddy could even react and take the kitten out of her way, she'd chased him under the bed. There was his place! The only one where he would be allowed to stay – tucked away in the corner. Poor Uddy, who was so afraid of the dark, given his terrible experience with the breeder! He'd expected a better welcome – wasn't this his so-called "forever home"? Oh, if only he could have stayed on the farm with Pegasus and Benedict. If only those pesky geese hadn't been around with their radio!

Harry tried to react, explain and scold (just a little, he was never good at scolding), but nothing helped. Tahiti took up position in front of the bed and growled every time the new kitten made the slightest movement. Her dad was obliged to close the bedroom door to keep her out whenever he needed to feed Uddy.

Two days passed, and there wasn't any improvement. Harry put the two cats in two separate carriers and took them to Mum's flat. Knowing Uncle Panda's peaceful nature, he hoped the wise old gentleman would be a mediator of peace and reconcile the kittens. That didn't happen, but Panda assumed the protective role. Whenever Tahiti wanted to launch an attack on Uddy, he would jump in the middle and shelter the little one with his large body. If needed, he would growl a bit to look more dissuasive. Tahiti, still very young, knew that she was no match for him. She would turn away, pretending to attack some random toy. Gradually, she realised that her attempts to subdue Uddy were doomed to failure and decided to ignore the black and white "nuisance," as she called him. Besides, Uddy grew very fast and quickly became more the subject of her admiration than a victim of her contempt. Nevertheless, the kittens never played together and avoided each other as much as possible. Harry was, of course, sorry he didn't have a cat in his flat anymore, so from time to time, he would take them both in for a weekend.

Mum told me a funny little story about one such sojourn.

One day, when the kitties had been on their "weekend" at Harry's, Mum visited to have tea with them. As she sipped her tea and chatted with her son, the two cats walked back and forth between the bedroom and the dining room. Mum, involved in the conversation, didn't pay much attention. Then, when it was time for her to leave, she noticed a pile of toys at her feet. The cats had been bringing them in, one by one. Both cats were sitting in front of their toys, looking insistently at Mum and meowing: "Mum, we are ready; let's go home!" No way Mum would go without them!

The message was clear, so Mum picked up the carrier, installed the two cats inside with some toys and left. The kitties were convinced that their natural home was now with Panda and Mum. Perhaps they sensed what was coming? Soon after, Harry had to move to another country for his job, and Tahiti and Uddy officially became Mum's cats.

A Round Belly

With three Maine Coons in the house, Mum thought this was the highest number of cats she could take care of. She had never wanted more than one cat; besides, her flat was tiny. However, neither Tahiti nor Uddy had been neutered, and they were both almost one year old. Mum was happy to proceed, but Harry was afraid the cats wouldn't reach their optimal size if neutered too early. The Maine Coons need almost five years to reach their maximum size, and if they are operated on too soon, their growth may stop. So, Mum waited and waited.

A little too long.

One day, she noticed Tahiti's round belly. Was she gaining weight or expecting babies? A visit to the vet confirmed the obvious: babies were in there, all impatient to discover Mum's flat, share toys and treats, plan mischief (obviously) and cause havoc.

"How many kittens is she expecting?" asked Mum, concerned about the future.

"Four, I believe," replied the vet after a quick examination.

"Forty," objected Tahiti, but fortunately, Mum wasn't listening.

"Four is fine. We can deal with four more kitties – it will be easy to find loving families for them."

How optimistic was Mum! And how the events that followed would prove her wrong! She had no idea what incredible changes the birth of the kittens would bring to her life.

The kittens were not four but eight: four sets of twins, four boys and four girls. Some were like two peas in a pod, others not quite identical. Mum says that Tahiti didn't notice she was expecting. Frightened, she forgot her firstborn under the bed, but Mum managed to save it, by only just.

Mum is very proud of having helped Tahiti through the birth process, especially since the young mother didn't know how to sever the umbilical cord. How did she manage to do it for the firstborn, the one she left under the bed? We don't know – anyway, she stopped doing it for the rest of the babies. Maybe she panicked and got tired. Perhaps she was too impressed by what was happening to her to participate. It was lucky Mum had done some research in advance and had everything ready: sterilised scissors, gauze, absorbent cotton, and so on.

The babies arrived at a relatively steady pace, and after three hours of teamwork, they were all born. Mum put the mother and her kittens into a clean, comfortable basket and prepared a good snack for the exhausted Tahiti.

I don't know if it's true, but Mum always claimed that Tahiti didn't like her before the babies were born. This changed after the birth. Likely grateful for her help, Tahiti became fond of Mum.

Very soon, it became clear that the young mother could not feed all the kittens; she could not produce enough milk to satisfy the eight hungry bellies, and the babies were crying all day long. In addition, she had rejected the last-born baby, a tiny black girl. Every time the little one came near her mum's belly,

Tahiti would push her away violently. The poor baby would drag herself to her mother's tail and roll into a ball resignedly.

Alarmed, Mum ran to the vet for advice. She came back loaded with boxes of powdered milk for kittens, bottles and instructions: the babies should be fed every two hours and the little "rejected" one every hour – day and night! As some were suckling very slowly, it was a non-stop job. Mum's flat became a nursery for the kittens. For three weeks, she hardly ever slept, neglected her office work and often forgot to eat. Fortunately, my human brother Harry had come home and was happy to lend a hand at that time.

However, another surprise awaited Mum. Early one morning, three weeks after the birth, she stepped into the room dedicated to the little family and found their basket empty! Where was Tahiti? What had happened to the babies? The room was utterly silent. After looking around frantically, she found a bundle of babies under a wardrobe, with their mother sitting proudly next to them. The stray cats always move their kittens to a safer place after a couple of weeks, but it was funny to see Tahiti carry her offspring just a few steps away. What danger could there be, in her own home? I don't remember our maman doing this with Caramel and me, probably because she felt we had already been through so much!

Looking for Names

Tahiti and Uddy, the kittens' parents, never took part in any cat shows. Mum didn't want them to be carried around, confined for days, handled by the judges, and so on.

"They are better off at home," she used to say. "They don't care for prizes and blue ribbons; all they need is love, good food and comfort."

However, the kittens' grandparents were both famous Maine Coons. Dad's dad, Rivers, was a European champion, and his mother, Steffi, won countless medals and ribbons. So, Mum wanted to provide continuity if this type of thing was essential to any future owners of the kittens. She registered the kittens with the breed registry, but in so doing, she had to respect some rules, especially regarding their names. That year, the letter V was designated for cats; thus, all cat names had to start with a V. It wasn't the easiest letter for names.

Mum watched the kittens for a few days before proceeding. What name would be suitable for this one? How should that one be named? As if the kittens would mind their names! Silly Mum. After some time spent head-scratching, she selected eight names she considered "acceptable." I would never have accepted any of them, but Mum has such strange taste!

The girls were named: Vanille, Vicky, Vivi and Valentina. The boys became Vlad, Vitalis, Vinci and Vito. Vito was a mutineer like me; he did not like his name. I am sure that he himself had suggested Maxi instead. It suited him very well; he had a big, round, funny head and a cheerful character.

Mum told us so many stories; some of the kittens have had incredible adventures. In the following few stories, I let her take the lead. Sometimes she tells it better than I do - well, only sometimes. And then, I wasn't born yet.

VINCI AND MAXI

BABY VALENTINA AND HER DAD UDDY

BABY VLAD

The Kitten Who Almost Died Twice

I let Mum tell you the story of Vanille, the firstborn of Tahiti's eight kittens.

When Tahiti went into labour, she didn't understand what was happening and got scared. First, she ran under the bed; then, she came to hide on my lap, hoping the pain would disappear. I quickly took her to the basket and settled her down the best I could, but I didn't know that she had already given birth to one of the kittens.

Once the kitty was comfortably installed, the babies started to arrive one after another. I was busy helping her; I needed to sever the cords as she seemed not to know how to do it. However, I kept catching a tiny noise coming from my bedroom - was the TV on? It couldn't be – it was four in the morning! Suddenly I got it: it must be a kitten! I hurried to check – the little cries were indeed coming from under my bed. I had to crawl under it to get the little one. Phew, I got there just in time! The tiny body was almost cold. I rubbed it with sterilised gauze and took it to its mother.

It was Vanille, the biggest of all newborns, a beauty. She didn't mind this oversight. As soon as the litter was complete, she appointed herself the commander-in-chief. When it turned out that Tahiti did not have enough milk, she was the first to accept the bottle and demonstrated how to do it to her brothers and sisters. Later on, she took the leading role in all the games they played and helped her mother keep everything in order in case of conflicts.

The kittens were all beautiful, but Vanille was gorgeous. When she was seven weeks old, the leading cat newspaper published her picture. The phone started to ring: everyone wanted Vanille. People were willing to buy her at "any price." They would say, "How much do you want for her? Name your price; it doesn't matter. We want to adopt her!"

But the kittens were not for sale, and besides, we decided that Vanille would never leave home.

This decision saved her life.

At six months, she started to have a persistent ear problem. The local vet diagnosed otitis, prescribed treatment and said she'd soon be better. But it went from bad to worse. We are fortunate to have the best clinic in the country only 15 minutes away from our home. The specialist who examined Vanille suspected a polyp had developed in her ear. The scanner exam confirmed the diagnosis and showed that the polyp had grown tremendously and wrapped itself around her left eye. A risky operation was needed.

The probability that it would fail was high; the life of our pretty little Vanille was at stake.

We had no choice – without the surgery, she would only have a few weeks to live, at best a few months. By incredible chance, a guest doctor was at the clinic at that time, a famous surgeon from the States. He was very interested in Vanille's case and took over her treatment with another surgeon.

I still remember that morning when I dropped her off at the clinic, not knowing if I would see her alive again. I didn't even want to go home! All morning, I wandered around the town in complete despair. Then finally, in the early afternoon, my mobile phone rang: the operation had been successful!

Vanille stayed in the clinic for six long days, most of the time on morphine. When I finally got her back, she was skeletal, as she had refused to eat in the hospital; her skull was still bandaged. They had cut off and removed her left ear but then sewn it on again.

When driving home, she tried desperately to put her little nose out between the carrier bars to give me kisses. She kept cuddling and licking my fingers.

Once back home, she recovered fast. Soon, she became our beautiful Vanille again, and it was impossible to guess that her ear had been sewn back on. Well, she's a bit deaf, but that doesn't matter.

The surgeons were as surprised as we were that the operation was successful. They called us every six months to check on Vanille's health for more than three years!

But the news we had to share with them was always excellent. Vanille had probably disliked her extended stay in the clinic so much that she had been careful not to get sick again.

BABY VANILLE

Sweet Little Angel

This is the story of my brother Maxi whom I never met. His registered name was Vito, but as he had a big round head and was a chubby baby, he was renamed Maxi.

I let Mum tell the story, although it's not easy for her.

Did Mummy cat Tahiti believe that Maxi was her firstborn? Is that why he was her favourite? Or did she sense what would eventually happen?

Maxi became her beloved baby, her precious little darling, from the moment he came into the world. All her love and attention were focused on that big black and white boy, and no one was allowed to touch him. If I ever wanted to take him out of the basket, Tahiti would growl, hiss and spit, ready to get her claws out. The young mother hardly paid any attention to her other kittens! She was too busy taking care of her little darling.

With so much love from his mother, one would expect him to be very attached to her, but he did not seem so. Sill a tiny kitten, he decided to explore the world, to have his own experiences. He moved out of the basket as early as the second week. One morning I found him with his brother Vlad on the cushion a little away from the basket. They were both sleeping peacefully, embracing each other.

They say there is an exceptional kitten in every litter, and Maxi was that one. He was cute, very affectionate and highly gregarious. The most active among the kittens, he participated in everyday life with enthusiasm and always wanted to "help" me. Was I back from shopping? Maxi was there to greet me and help me put the groceries away. Was it time to cook? He had to assist! He sat at the kitchen table and carefully observed every move, to be trained for later when grown up. He probably wanted to become a famous Chef. And whenever I made pancake batter, Maxi, like a kid, wanted to join in; he would put one of his front paws in the batter and start mixing it. He would take it out and shake it vigorously as soon as I noticed. He didn't mind going under the shower after that; he was so sweet and trusted me so much that he would have followed me to the world's end.

Clever as the most intelligent dog, he understood many words and always wanted to take part in conversations and share his adventures with the visitors. He would talk to everybody all day long. Anyone who came to the house was captivated by him.

When visitors arrived, whether Maxi knew them or not, he would greet them with profuse joy, inquire about their health and well-being, and sit down to share a cup of tea and a chat. He would immediately reply when someone talked to him, tilting his head from side to side in approval, kneading and purring joyfully. He was funny, and it was heart-warming to look at him.

Visitors always wanted to leave with Maxi in their arms – or at least with his photo. Frequently they called back to inquire after him. "How is Maxi?" was the first question they would ask, not "how are the kitties?" or "how are you?"

All his siblings loved him. His twin brother, Vinci, took it upon himself to be his guardian angel. He followed him everywhere and watched him like a loving mother. Whenever Maxi allowed it, he would wash his fur and spread kisses on his head. Daddy Uddy taught him all the foolish and no-no things to do, and they became perfect disorder-creating companions. Vlad, whom Maxi admired above all, became his sports coach. Unfortunately for Maxi, it often ended in a plunge! Vlad is a perfect athlete, while Maxi was rather chubby.

Kittens engaged in games, and sometimes they were rough and tumble. When there was too much noise or quarrels, Mummy Tahiti jumped in the middle and smacked everyone. With one exception: she would lift her paw to apply the hit on the next kitten, then she stopped, noticing the next was her beloved darling Maxi. Of course, it was never his fault!

When it was time to sleep, he would run into my bedroom. Sitting in front of the bed, he would call me, urging me to come. "Meow, are you coming yet? What are you doing?! I'm waiting!"

Only when I was lying down would he jump next to me and stretch his body all along my arm, holding me with his paws. He slept like a baby all night without ever moving.

Maxi was our happy little chap. Adorable little clown, he brought sunshine into the house and embellished our life. Little birdie, he would talk and sing and jump and play all day long all over the place.

Every day was a celebration for Maxi. It was as if he knew how short his life would be, and he wanted to benefit from every second of it, day after day.

It happened one beautiful spring day, around noon. I had just arrived back from shopping, and as usual, there was something special in my basket for Maxi. He spotted it, jumped on his small round table in the kitchen where he used to eat - and waited to be served, chatting with me. After a cuddle session to thank me, he started to feast, with great enthusiasm, as always. I left the kitchen to attend to my chores when suddenly I heard a terrible cry. Rushing back, I found Maxi in great pain – his back paw was visibly aching. He couldn't walk.

I thought he had a sprain, so I put him in the carrier and took him to the nearby vet.

"This is very serious," said the vet. "It's probably an embolism." He directed me to the best clinic in the country, which is only 15 min drive away.

Sadly, the diagnosis was confirmed. Maxi received morphine to ease his pain and stayed in the clinic for further treatment.

I was distressed - I would give my life for my little treasure! I called the vet clinic several times a day in the following days. His condition was stable; I desperately hoped he would eventually get better and return home. I couldn't sleep. I couldn't eat. Every minute of the day or night, I thought of my darling little Maxi, shut in a cage in the clinic, probably suffering.

The bad news arrived a few days later: Maxi had gone over the rainbow bridge. He had grown too fast, and his heart, probably weak from birth, could not take it. At 16 months, Maxi was the same size as his giant dad Uddy, whereas Maine Coons reach their full size at four or five years of age.

Mummy cat Tahiti couldn't understand why her beloved son hadn't returned. She had seen him in the carrier as he was about to leave and rushed to help him. She had seen me carrying him away through the kitchen window. He'll be back. Eventually, she thought. She sat by that window for weeks, looking out, calling softly. He cannot go away; he cannot break the thread of love that united them.

But he didn't come. For weeks his mother cat refused to feed herself properly, barely eating, and I started to worry for her.

Then something happened.

One stormy night, I returned home carrying a little black and white kitten inside my handbag.

* * *

Freddy here, dear reader. Let me tell you this part, Mum, please!

It was me, inside the handbag! After searching for days, Mum finally found me on the pavement and picked me up. As soon as Mummy Tahiti saw me, she rushed to take care of me. She licked my wet fur to dry me, gave me cuddles and kisses to comfort me, and hugged me next to her belly to warm me. She purred to make me feel at home, "My son," she murmured, "my dear little son!"

Of course, she knew I wasn't her beloved Maxi, but she believed I was a present granted to her from heaven. As soon as I entered the house, I became her new baby, her new little darling, and she was happy again.

Knowing how much Maxi's story had affected them all, I try to do everything to make them happy again. I jump and run around the house every day. I roll around and sing my happy meows, pretend to be silly, chase my tail and play "the little clown", just to see them smiling and laughing.

I know that nothing and nobody could ever replace Maxi. But Mum said one day we will all be together somewhere over the rainbow bridge. And we will waltz around, and it will be the most beautiful and happy dance one has ever seen.

I don't know where this place is, but Mum said it's far, far away and we don't have to worry. We just have to live and be as happy as we can be.

MAXI

No Better Place Than Home

Sometimes there are extraordinary coincidences in life. If it weren't for Vicky's terrible adventure, I wouldn't be alive today. Yet it happened before I was even born. I'll let mum tell you the whole story.

If you remember from one of the former stories, I intended to find loving families for some of Tahiti's kittens. My flat was far too small for 11 Maine Coons. And I was reluctant to move – the apartment was lovely, with beautiful views and very conveniently located. I also thought some of the kittens would be happier as only cats in their own homes, especially boys who were all dominant cats. Thus, three of them, Vinci, Vlad and Vitalis, went away, apparently very happy to leave, especially the last two. I had daily news from their families, and the kittens reigned supreme in their new kingdoms. Anyway, I was sorry to let them go and still am today.

Vicky should be the next one. She was solitary and didn't mix with others. The only exception was her twin sister Vivi, whom Mummy Tahiti had rejected at birth. In some way, Vicky had replaced their mother, providing care and education. Maybe I didn't pay enough attention to this fact. I thought that my beautiful Vicky would be happier as the only cat. And I certainly didn't understand Vicky's love, her silent attachment to her family. Ah, if only Freddy had been there! He would have warned me; he is such an intuitive little chap. But back then, he wasn't even born yet.

Impossible Dilemma

I had had several conversations with a woman from the Ardennes (north-eastern France) who wanted to provide a home for a Maine Coon kitten. She saw Vicky's photos in a cat magazine and fell in love with her. After many phone calls and tons of explanations from both sides, I thought we could give it a try. She seemed a trustworthy person who would be able to take care of Vicky and love her. She and her family lived in a house with a spacious garden. They were already building fences to secure it so that Vicky wouldn't wander into the nearby forest. There was a slight drawback, though: she had two young children. But she said they loved cats and were looking forward to Vicky's arrival.

I remembered that Saturday as if it would happen yesterday. It was mid-July and the hottest day of the year. We had set up a meeting for the early afternoon.

"Come around two o'clock", I said.

But the woman and her husband rang our door at 11 am. They were too impatient to get Vicky. Good sign, I thought, although I would have preferred to have another couple of hours with my little girl. Anyhow, there was nothing to do but welcome them.

I don't remember where all the kitties were at the time, but when they walked into the living room, Vicky was the only one present, sleeping on the sofa. Hearing the visitors, she jumped up, came to me, and rubbed against my legs. They wanted to cuddle her, but Vicky hid under my long skirt. She was seeking protection. This was unusual behaviour for her - and I got a bit alarmed. Although she was not notably affectionate with her siblings, she was always friendly with visitors and wasn't afraid of anyone. Now, she stayed close to me, sheltering around my legs and avoiding the couple.

We chatted a bit and had a few refreshing drinks. As I was reluctant to let the kitten leave directly, I invited them for lunch at a nearby Italian restaurant.

Throughout the meal, I desperately searched for the politest way to say, "Look, I've changed my mind. Sorry, but Vicky doesn't seem at ease with you, and I can't let her go."

I should have had the courage to do it, to say it. It would have spared us a lot of the heartache that was to come on both sides and pain to the poor kitty.

But how could I tell this to people who had travelled five hours on a hot day and were so happy to get their new cat? They kept telling me about all the little things they had done at home to get it ready for her so that she would feel at ease. I hardly listened, though. A tiny voice kept telling me that Vicky and this couple were incompatible.

When we got back to the flat, Vicky seemed more relaxed and even let herself be cuddled by the woman. Maybe my hunch was wrong? Perhaps it was just my torment at seeing another kitten leave?

Anyway, we signed Vicky's adoption papers, installed her in the carrier, and after the last kiss, I said goodbye to her. She raised her head and looked at me with her expressive, smart eyes, and I could read what she was saying: "Mum, I want to stay with you!"

But I let her go, with tears in my eyes.

The whole afternoon I waited impatiently for their phone call. How went the trip? Hadn't Vicky suffered too much from the heat? Did she like her new home?

The telephone finally rang late in the evening. The news was somewhat reassuring: Vicky was sitting between her new Dad and Mum and purring. She had accepted a bit of water but had not yet wanted anything to eat.

Maybe that was normal. After all, the kitty had just endured a four-hour trip on a scorching day in a car without air conditioning, and the new surroundings would undoubtedly have disturbed her. I thought she would be better in a day or two, and everything would be fine.

I let four or five days go by. I didn't want to sound intrusive, but I was impatient to get news. Then I called, genuinely expecting to be comforted.

Bad News

So you can imagine my shock when I learnt that the kitten had refused to eat anything since she had left her home! All she had consumed daily was water and a few drops of milk. It was worrying as she was a big gourmand and liked all kinds of food.

I felt during the conversation that the woman was distraught; she told me she had taken the kitten to the vet and got some appetite stimulants. I wasn't pleased about this – Vicky was a robust cat, the biggest girl in the litter, and had left her home in perfect health. Giving her medication when she didn't need any would only disrupt her growth. I immediately emailed a list of Vicky's favourite foods and treats, and we agreed to talk a week later.

But I couldn't wait a week. After three days, I called back, worried and distressed.

The situation was the same. Vicky wasn't eating – she was living on water and small amounts of milk. Her health had started to suffer: she was becoming thinner, and her fur had lost its shine.

I asked several questions about their household - were there any changes since Vicky's arrival? The woman told me they had another cat, an adopted stray who had just given birth to six kittens. I had explicitly inquired whether there were any other cats in the household before she came to fetch Vicky, and she said none! If I had known the truth, I would not have let Vicky go with them. She didn't even fit in well with her own feline family, so with an unknown cat. . . And now the kittens, too! This would have upset her even more as she had a very developed maternal instinct. At home, she was always looking after her stuffed mice; she would carry them to the water bowl and place them on the plate of biscuits so that they could "feed" themselves. Seeing a mother cat surrounded by her kittens must have disturbed her.

I advised the woman to separate the two cats and keep Vicky in a room where the other cat had no access, at least for a short time. I hoped Vicky would calm down and start accepting food.

A few days later, I called back, expecting to hear that there had been at least a slight improvement. It had been over three weeks since Vicky had left me. How could she not have eaten all this time? How could she survive on only water and some milk?

As soon as the woman heard my voice, she started to cry. The cat was getting worse and worse; she wasn't accepting any food and was now barely able to move.

She had concluded that the kitten was seriously ill and took her to another vet, a specialist. The vet had prescribed another treatment and given Vicky a few injections of who knows what.

I was distressed. What was this woman doing with my beautiful, healthy kitty? It was clear the poor baby needed to get back home urgently. I had already suggested this several times, and the woman always refused. Now, it was getting serious, kitty's life was at stake. We could come any time to fetch the cat and were willing to reimburse her for all the expenses she had incurred and compensate her for her care, I said. She refused; she still hoped that things would work out and that the cat would finally decide to eat.

From that point on, I started to become seriously worried.

All I could think of, all day long, was Vicky. When I called again in the evening, I shuddered in anticipation of more bad news. The situation lasted two more weeks – I called every evening and there was nothing but crying on both sides of the line. Yet, she wasn't willing to return Vicky to me.

It was then that I decided that no more kittens would leave my home. I started to look for a house with a garden where we could all live together. But what I wanted most of all was to see my Vicky back home.

One evening very late the telephone rang. It was the woman. She was crying so much that she could hardly speak. I feared the worst. Finally, she told me in between sobs that the kitty had reached the end of her life. She wouldn't make it through the night.

What terrible news! But you know what, Freddy? I didn't believe it. Whenever someone tells me that one of my kitties is seriously ill or will die, I don't accept it. For me, this is unthinkable, hence impossible.

"Don't do anything! Don't take any action! Don't take her to any vet, don't give her any medicine," I said to the lady. "We'll come first thing in the morning and take her home."

Strangely enough, I wasn't worried anymore. Now that the woman had finally agreed to give Vicky back to me, everything would be fine. I was sure of that.

The next day at dawn (I think it was four in the morning), my son got into his car. He set off for the Ardennes, a chequebook in his pocket, ready to reimburse the family for every conceivable expense. I didn't care about the money; all I wanted was to have my little girl back home.

Coming Home

My son arrived with Vicky mid-afternoon. He told me that he had found her small black body sitting on a heater, her eyes closed, apparently not reacting to anything. But as soon as she heard his voice, she opened her eyes, and "it was as if two little stars had lit up inside," he said. It made him so happy! The kitten recognised him; she knew he had come to take her back!

Vicky was in a terrible state. Once one of the most beautiful Maine Coon among Tahiti's kittens, she was now a tiny, skeletal thing. Her fur, or at least what was left of it, was dull and grey and coming off in clumps. In addition, she had sores all over her body, especially on her head. Had she been mistreated? Perhaps the kids had done something to her secretly without letting their parents see. I still believed that they had genuinely loved her. Had she been bitten, attacked by the other cat? I would never know, and I didn't want to call them back.

That same day, I showed her to our usual vet, who concluded that she was indeed seriously ill and prescribed long-term treatment. Again, I listened to him and did not believe a word. For safety, however, I kept her isolated during that night. I offered her some food, but she wouldn't accept any.

The next day, I took her to the famous clinic, the one where they had saved Vanille. A specialist checked the kitty thoroughly, spending a lot of time with her, and finally declared: "There is nothing wrong with this cat. Just put her with her brothers and sisters, and she will start eating."

That was precisely what I had thought but had been too scared to try, given her terrible state. Happy and relieved, I returned home, brought the carrier with Vicky directly into the living room and freed her. Instantly the room became a place of celebration! All kitties gathered around her and greeted her with a profusion of joy. They circled her and meowed happily; everyone wanted to give her a nose kiss. Slowly, she started to respond, sniffed them, and rubbed her head on their fur. The room was full of purring - it sounded like a giant engine was running nearby.

Once the greeting had been done correctly, as it should be after more than one month of absence, she walked straight to the plate of cat biscuits and started to eat. Slowly at first, then with increasing appetite. I thought she would never stop! I kept pulling her preferred food out of the fridge: treats, cheese, ham, anything she liked. It was such a pleasure to look at her! I again had tears in my eyes, but they were tears of joy. When she finally stopped eating, she found her preferred basket and settled for a nice nap. I'm sure it was her first happy nap for many weeks.

I knew from the start there was nothing wrong with my kitty. I think she had decided to come back home whatever it takes, probably as soon as the couple walked through our door. And no matter if that meant putting her life at risk. Clever and wise, she had probably felt she couldn't cover the long journey back home by escaping, so the only choice she had was to go on a hunger strike. Humans do it when pushed to their limit. Vicky taught me that cats could do it too.

It didn't even take a month for her to become what she had been before leaving us – a beautiful Maine Coon kitten, our little star, one of the most beautiful in our house. Her behaviour also reverted to what it had been before. It seemed she had not been affected by her terrible ordeal.

Four Lives Saved at a Time

When Mum stopped talking, I realised how much Vicky's story affected our life, my Maman's, Caramel's and mine. Without that dreadful event, Mum would never start to look for a new house. She would stay in her little flat and wouldn't know anything about the vacant lot, a black kitty and her two kids who desperately needed her help.

But due to this dramatic adventure, she decided to keep all her kitties and started looking for a house with a garden. By an incredible coincidence, she had found one just down the road from the vacant lot, where our Maman would have given birth to us only a few months later. In a way, Vicky had saved her own life and ours, simultaneously.

VICKY

Chapter Three

In which a garden becomes magic, Freddy gets new brothers and sisters, and a kitty decides to go away. And a tiny hedgehog gets himself a new mum. To say nothing about a dog - oops, a cat who believes she is a dog.

The House on the Corner

A large ginger and white cat was squatting in the gardens around the park. They were his kingdom; at least, that's what he believed. His properties extended as far as the eye could see, that is, over four gardens around the corner house. Although his kingship was self-proclaimed, you'd better believe he was a royal. Otherwise, you'd better be able to run very, very fast.

No one knew how long he had lived there or where he came from – not even himself. Mum may know more, but she is such a lousy storyteller that I don't even want to ask her! He had no one to care for him and no cat biscuits other than those he found spilt on the ground by some overindulged fat cat neighbour.

His name was "the cat", although he was also described as the dirty cat, vagabond, scoundrel, pirate, and similar. It was all because of his bad manners – he used to steal food and overturn garbage bins with the help of his friend and neighbour, the fox who lived in the park. But oh, what else could he do? One needs to eat at least a few times a week. I can vouch for that! I had suffered so much hunger when I was tiny!

Fortunately, one person in his kingdom was kind to him – the old man who lived in the house on the corner, which is where this story begins.

The cat believed him to be a piano player. Still, Mum said he was a retired engineer and a passionate musician. You could hear Meowzart or Barkhoven or even Ratmaninov masterpieces echoing through the garden for days on end. It sometimes happened – although seldom – that he would stop playing, look out of the window and notice the cat.

"Hungry, buddy, aren't you?" he would call down to him, and then he would pop into his kitchen in search of a few titbits.

Ah, what the heck! That lousy fridge was empty most of the time. Not only did the old man lack money for groceries, but filled with dreams of music, he would also often forget to go shopping! However, every now and then, there would be leftover chicken or some stale bread. Happy and relieved, the old man would place them on a saucer and take them into the garden as treats for the cat.

"Come, my friend, have a feast!" He would then have called.

The cat would not rush to them – he knew how to behave. We cats are masters when it comes to expressing gratitude! First, he would look up at the old man. Then he would rub his head against his legs and purr the most beautiful cat concerto, much more harmonious than anything the famous Meowzart had ever written. Ha! I'm sure he will want to copy it one day, this musician. What, Mum? He died long ago? Well, precisely, of jealousy. One can never compete with a cat.

The cat would then grab a piece of chicken or bread, take it to the bamboo hedge and start to eat. Very slowly. Because he knew that when there is not much on the plate, you have to chew each mouthful carefully to savour it. I did this too before I met Mum.

In those moments, he would feel happy and almost, almost loved. Someone had taken notice of him.

Someone had offered him food. Well, of course, it wasn't much, but it was much more than he was used to.

Such was the life of the ginger and white cat. He wandered through his vast estate of the four gardens surrounding the corner house; he slept here and there, mainly under a random car parked on the street. He ate what he could find, and if he couldn't find anything, he would go to see the old man.

Farewell

But life is a rocky road; one day, the old man disappeared. It was around lunchtime on a Sunday. The roast chicken was on the old man's menu and the cat got plenty of leftovers. Was it a farewell present?

After the meal, the old man took his rusty bicycle out of the garage, dusted it off, and said to the cat: "I'll leave you in charge of the house. Be good! I'll be back tonight, and maybe we'll have another feast." You see, it was the old man's birthday.

He moved the broken garden gate, mounted his steed and disappeared down the road to Paris.

The cat had waited for him that evening until late. He waited for him the next day and the day after that. Then the whole week and the week that followed. But the piano had fallen silent; there were no more melodious sounds rolling through the garden, no more bread or chicken leftovers. No matter how patiently the cat waited or how many times he stood in front of the garden gate looking down the street leading to Paris, the old man never returned.

Maybe he was sitting on the terrace of some lovely café, having forgotten the promise he'd made to the cat? Parisian cafés are so charming, you know! Or maybe he was hanging out around the Opera House – as Mum often does. Or maybe he drove too fast on his old bike? The mayor of Paris has the police stop anyone who exceeds snail's pace.

Frankly, I wonder why the cat didn't go to Paris himself to enquire. I would do it. It's so easy. A direct route leads from the house on the corner straight to the city centre. They call it the "green path". Once, a long time ago, it was a track for another terrible yellow monster – the "high-speed train". But it roared too loud, and even before I was born, they decided to bury it underground. They heard I'm going to be afraid of yellow monsters, such kind people! Instead, they built a path so that we cats can run to the city centre safely and window-shop. You know, not many of us can afford more. Ah, Paris is such an expensive city!

I would have run on the path, straight to the Opera House, to search for the old man and asked everyone, "Have you seen a piano player on a rusty bike?"

"Yes, of course," they would reply, "He's right there!" and point me to the big stairs. The old man would be sitting on the steps of the Opera House, reading a score, his rusty bike laid at his feet.

"Uncle," I would say, "you forgot to come home!"

"Home?" he would reply. "Where is that?"

I would then set him on his bike and run in front of him to show him the way back. Back to the house on the corner, to my place. Or, more precisely, to the house that would soon be mine. But that came later.

Only, even though the ginger and white cat may have been a self-proclaimed king, he was like many leaders: he had no sense of initiative. Not knowing what to think or what to do after the old man's departure, he went to the park to seek advice from his friend, the fox, who had been appointed the prime minister of the cat's kingdom.

"Of course, he'll come back!" asserted the prime minister, who knew everything about nothing. "He went shopping in Paris! He'll soon return with loads of tuna cans and tons of chicken breasts!"

Just imagine. When the cat heard this, he started salivating right away! A feast? He hadn't eaten in days! It was worth waiting for. He quickly ran back to the garden to not miss the old man's return.

But oh, what a disappointment. Instead of his friend, the musician, men in blue arrived and clattered up the garden with much unnecessary stuff – cement bags, piles of wood, paint cans and the like.

"Workers," said the prime minister, who had become an expert in modern architecture for this occasion. "They will make that old shack into a stylish house, you'll see!"

The cat didn't care about the style of the house. Besides, there was no point in hanging around. The work went on and on. The noise was unbearable, to say nothing about the dust! Also, the workers didn't leave anything edible in the garden except greasy sandwich papers.

But one day . . .

It was early morning. The cat had just returned from a big party in the park. He and the fox had unearthed a particularly well-stocked bin the night before - a feast! They had invited all the stray cats from the neighbourhood and squirrels from the park. The party had lasted until the early hours.

Actually, the cat was under the influence as there was plenty of condensed milk at the party. His ideas weren't really crystal clear. And when he heard the sound of a big engine in front of the house, he became afraid.

"A tiger! A yellow tiger!"

The engine was indeed yellow with big black letters, Mum told us later. Moreover, it looked straight at the cat with its enormous eyes (the headlights were on as it was still dark). It all seemed very frightening indeed. But oh, wasn't he silly. Mistaking it for a tiger! I would know right away what it was: a yellow monster!

He ran, belly to the ground, and hid in the bamboo hedge. Not that he was a coward – no! It was just that a few cans of condensed milk could turn your head.

As soon as he came to his senses and the day began to dawn, he understood it all. The old man had returned! The fox was right; the old man had only been shopping in the city! Here he was again with tons of canned tuna, loads of roast chicken and who knows what all the other wonders were in the countless crates, bags and boxes! Workers were carrying them from the truck-tiger to the house all day long. What else could be inside? Ah, probably ham – boiled, smoked, grilled – all sorts of ham!

But one small thing worried him: where was he, the old man? The cat had not seen him all day long. Nor had he heard a single note from the piano! Ah, maybe he was too busy unpacking.

The cat waited patiently until dusk. Then the tiger started to roar again. It turned on its huge yellow eyes and carried the men off into the night.

Time for dinner, thought the cat. He dashed to the front door, his tail straight and high. "Meow, meow!" he called as he ran across the lawn. "I'm here! I've come to help unpack!" Indeed, the poor old man would badly need his help. Just imagine a house full of food!

He reached the front door – but then, what a surprise!

Big Head

What was that? On the other side of the front glass door, a giant cat's head watched him. "Pffft," hissed the ginger cat. "Pfff, pfft!"

But instead of backing away, the other one kept meowing in the kindest tones. "Meow." And once again, "meow, meow!"

Cheeky guy; he's welcoming me! Thought the cat. *Who does he think he is? That place is my kingdom. I don't need a welcome!*

Before he could decide whether to walk away, the door opened, and Mum stepped out. She told us later that it had been their first evening in the new house. She was getting dinner ready when she heard my uncle Panda calling someone from the hallway. She came to see what was going on and what she saw was pretty funny, she said. There were two enormous cats' heads opposite each other; one inside (Panda's) and one outside (ginger and white cat's), pressing their noses against the glass door.

Mum was so happy there was a cat! She'd asked the former owners whether they had a cat, and they had said no. Of course, she had been deceived. But look at this, there was a cat! She quickly ran to the kitchen to fetch something good for him. A few minutes later, she stepped out with a large bowl of cat biscuits.

The cat backed away a bit but didn't leave; he was too hungry. But he was worried. Was this lady going to chase him away? That's what people usually do. Was this bowl of food really for him, or was it for that guy from inside who stepped out with her?

"Hello, kitty!" said Mum. "Don't be afraid! Look, we brought your dinner! I'm Mum, and this guy here is Panda."

The cat looked at both of them with wide eyes. Mum? What was this name? What does this mean? He had never heard this word before. And that strange guy was called Panda - what a ridiculous name! After all, it didn't matter; he had a bowl of cat biscuits right at his paws, so he started to devour them. They tasted so good! He had almost finished when suddenly he heard Mum talking to him.

"Kitty, you have such a large head! You know, we are going to call you Big Head!"

The cat was startled; this was outrageous! He should have expected it - had she not called her cat Panda? He was so annoyed that he ignored the last two or three biscuits. I quite understand him; I would have been vexed too! Big Head? What a name!

Given the outrage, the cat decided to leave the garden immediately. He trotted off without further ado, neither a goodbye nor a thank-you, his tail high in the air. *That'll teach them*, he thought. *Calling me*

Big Head! How is that a name for the king of the gardens, I ask you?

"Goodbye!" shouted Mum as he reached the hedge. "Come back tomorrow!"

"Ha, come back tomorrow! They won't see me again," the cat mumbled as he jumped over the fence. He was going to the park to complain to his friend, the fox. Err, I mean the prime minister.

He didn't have to go far because the fox was on his way to the house on the corner.

Magic Biscuits

"You know, the old man has come back." The cat was so annoyed that he'd got a bit confused.

"You see, I told you!" We all feel proud when it appears we've guessed something right, and the fox was no different.

"Yes, but it's not exactly him. It's Mum!"

Eh? Wasn't the fox right then? "Mum? What's that – who's that?" The cat might be rambling. Had the return of the old man confused him so much?

"Mum is a lady who gives out cat biscuits."

How strange, thought the fox, but who cares? "Biscuits? Are they good? Are there any left? Let's go and check!"

"Better be careful, my friend! She also gives out ridiculous names!" warned the cat. He told his friend about his brand-new name. As expected, the fox burst out laughing. He laughed so hard that he would roll around if it wasn't for those biscuits waiting for him.

"You, Big Head! I can't believe it! But my friend, you are the pirate, the brigand of all the gardens, the. . ."

"The king," corrected the cat, increasingly offended. It was not a good day for him. He should have stayed in bed.

Then suddenly, the fox stopped laughing.

"But wait a minute. . . Big Head. . . That's a very flattering name!"

"You think so?" The cat was doubtful.

"Of course it is! It makes you think of someone very learned! A smart cat who knows everything – well, not as learned as myself, but quite sufficient for a cat!"

"For a king," corrected the cat, who did not allow any deviation from his royal status.

"Oh, stop sulking, and let's go back to the garden," suggested the fox.

When they arrived in the garden of the corner house, they found the bowl filled to the brim with biscuits. Without really noticing it, they started to eat together, muzzle to muzzle, pushing each other lightly. They raced to see who could grab the most enormous batch. But the cat soon felt that his belly was too full and surrendered the bowl to his friend. He sat next to the fox, licking the top of his head from time to time to encourage him to eat more.

Then, once the bowl was empty, which happened very quickly with the fox's gluttony, they sat down on the wooden bench to chat for a while. It was a cold night, so they huddled together to keep warm.

"You left a lot of biscuits. Thank you, my friend." The fox dipped his muzzle into the cat's fur and rubbed it a little like a token of thanks.

The cat suddenly remembered that the bowl had been almost empty when he had left the garden.

"It's strange," he said, "I thought – indeed, I'm sure – that I finished almost all the biscuits. Only two or three were left at the bottom of the bowl."

"Ah, you must have been dreaming."

"No, it's true! I can even tell you what picture was at the bottom: it was a little bear."

"Really? Let's check!"

The fox took the bowl in his mouth and carried it further into the garden, where the street lamp lit the lawn as it was already dark.

"It's true; there is a tiny bear in red trousers on the bottom of the bowl."

"Ah, you see!"

"But then, how come there were so many biscuits? The bowl was full!"

Amazed, they returned to the bench to mull it over. After a long silence, the fox had an idea:

"What if they were magic biscuits?"

"What do you mean, magic?" The cat didn't understand the word "magic". First, the fox didn't know how to explain it. He thought and thought and finally concluded:

"If the biscuits are magic, then the whole garden is magic! And this means the food will always be available here from now on. You know, Big Head, my friend, I'll take all my dinners here."

He thought a little longer and added: "And maybe also my lunches!"

The cat looked around. Who was the fox talking to? Big Head? Then he remembered – it was his new name! Finally, it sounded great, so he decided he loved it.

They agreed to meet the next day at dinner time – same place, same hour – to taste those wonderful magic cat biscuits again.

A Garden Full of Cats

When they arrived the evening after, what a surprise. The garden was full of cats!

Nobody knew how or when exactly the news had spread. In the garden of that big house on the corner, there was a first-class cat restaurant, went the rumour. It was said to be open seven days a week, 24 hours daily and all year round. There was an all-you-can-eat buffet at your disposal, and roast chickens flew around, ready to land on your plate whenever you lifted a paw. To say nothing about the salmon and grilled tuna. And ham! Imported for cats directly from Spain, cooked in honey and served with creamy spaghetti!

Of course, the news attracted all the cats in the surroundings, even those whose existence was only suspected until then.

Fake news, dear reader, but you know how a rumour goes. It was all because of those magic biscuits.

However, there was food for everyone as Mum had laid out saucers of cat biscuits and other treats on the large garden table. Thus, when Big Head and the fox arrived, a crowd of cats welcomed them.

And evening after evening, the cats would gather in the Magic Garden. It has become a fashionable spot, where you had to be seen, even if you weren't hungry. A social venue where kitties could talk and exchange news, where stories are told and shared late at night. Of course, all this after a hearty feast and a creamy "catpuccinno" at the coffee bar. Err, I mean a bit of water lapping at the jar.

At first, Big Head didn't want to accept the new order of things and tried to shoo everyone away. He was the king here, wasn't he? However, even if he chased them away from one side of the garden, the cheeky kitties would get back from the other side. After Mum set up a cosy basket just for him on the terrace, he got used to the new rules.

I don't want to say that he suddenly became sweet since he still chases me. Often. But when I complain, he pretends it's just for play.

As for the old man, you may ask, what happened to him? He remained with his son in Paris because, he said, he was too old to get on his bike and ride back home. I still plan to go to the Opera House one day and bring him back, even if the house is no longer his.

You know, it's mine now. Shortly after Mum bought the house and moved in, she found me on the pavement and brought me to my forever home.

Now it's called Freddy's house on the corner, and if you ever pass by, you will know why there are so many cats in the garden.

It's because it's magic, my Magic Garden.

BIG HEAD

Four Black Elves

One morning, Mum and I saw my black Maman relaxing in the garden alley. No one had seen her for several weeks. She'd disappeared after realising that Mum wanted to trap her and take her to the vet to "spay" her. My Maman didn't want that to happen, especially since she'd just found a new boyfriend (as we later came to understand).

It was such a delight to see Maman again! I started to run all around the garden like a crazy kitty, jumping over the flower beds, climbing the big maple tree and scaring our two blackbirds, just for a laugh. But I didn't dare get too close to Maman! If you remember, the last time I did, she asked me not to follow her in a . . . well . . . in a bit harsh way. But just seeing her again, knowing she was in the garden, was such a joy!

However, I was a bit worried about her. She had an enormous belly!

"Mum, look, my Maman has eaten too many biscuits! Is she going to get sick?"

Mum laughed, but I saw that she, too, was worried.

"Freddy, her belly is full of little kittens," she said. "Your sisters and brothers!"

I loved that! Of course, I had plenty of brothers and sisters in the house in the form of the Maine Coons. But only uncle Panda was allowed to come into the garden, and besides, he wasn't very playful. What a delightful perspective! To see my brothers and sisters running on the lawn, playing hide and seek, climbing on the wisteria and the trees, exploring the vast bamboo hedge or just resting in the shade on the terrace with me! I hoped that there would be at least a hundred of them! And I wanted them all to be black like my Maman. Isn't it the most beautiful colour for a cat?

That same day, Mum started to explore the garden. "Freddy," she said, "where would your Mum like to get her new house? She needs one for her new kittens. We don't have a fir tree like the one you had in the vacant lot, and the bamboo hedge is too dark and humid. And if it rains, she will not be safe anywhere. Do you think your Maman would like to go into the garage?"

I had no idea, but Mum said it would need to be a pretty private place, not easy to find. Once, when she was little, Mum had had a wildcat from the forest, and she'd learned how protective untamed cats are of their babies. She knew my Maman wouldn't want to show her little ones to anyone until she felt they were old enough to face the world.

Mum kept searching in the garden for the perfect spot. As for me, I helped: I ate all the cat biscuits that were left on the garden table.

Mum laughed instead of appreciating my help – I wonder why?

"Freddy", she said "You know what? I think we'll get ready a few cosy baskets here and there; then, it will be up to your Maman to choose one. Do you agree?"

We went into the cellar and collected a few crates and plastic baskets (you can't leave a fabric box outside, said Mum). Then we went to Mum's wardrobe and picked out several old pullovers to line them and make them cosy. I wanted to take a beautiful pink pullover, but Mum said it was a brand-new cashmere, and she loved it.

FREDDY'S "MAMAN"

We tried to find the most agreeable spots in the garden (I sniffed them to check they were comfortable). By the end of the day, there were two baskets hidden in the hedges, each protected with branches and lined with a soft pullover. My favourite had an umbrella roof! We also put one on the terrace, where Maman would be sheltered from the rain and the wind. I hoped so much that she would fall for this one! The fourth one was in the garage. Maman could always sneak inside through a half-opened window.

Of course, I tested them all and can confirm that they were pretty comfortable!

Maman kept coming into the garden for breakfast, lunch, snacks, and dinner in the following week. Usually, she stayed a bit, resting close to the house and basking in the sun before leaving. She was never interested in our basket installations. However, I did all I could to draw her attention to them. I wonder if she even noticed them.

Then she disappeared again for several days, and I got worried. Mum said, "The big day is coming, Freddy!" She inspected our baskets' installation, but they were all empty. Only the umbrella roof one got a tenant: a hedgehog mum had found it to her liking and moved in with her babies. Mum let her stay.

"The rent is free, and dinner is included," she said and went to fetch a plate of biscuits as a welcome present.

It was maybe four or five days later that I saw Maman again. She seemed very tired yet in a great hurry to leave. She quickly swallowed the dinner that had been set out for her. Mum said it was extra rich – roast chicken, tuna, and cat milk with cream. As she was leaving, Maman grabbed a piece of chicken to take with her for later.

I was disappointed that she hadn't brought any babies! Not even one of them. Wasn't I their big brother? I hoped she'd do it the next time she visited. But she had not done so, although she came every day to eat.

In the meantime, Mum had kept looking. Where was the new babies' home? Where had Maman found shelter this time? Mum would have liked to help her, take food to her home to avoid the dangers on the road and the fear of leaving the little ones alone. Who knew what could happen? But all Mum's searches were in vain. However, Mum wasn't too worried this time. And she was right. Soon, Maman started to fetch food several times a day to feed the babies.

"You know, Freddy," Mum said, "I don't think your Maman is far away."

I thought so, too, because sometimes, she would come back for another little piece of food only a few minutes after leaving. I would have followed her, but Mum said she might carry the babies further away if disturbed. And that, of course, I didn't want! All I wanted was to have them here, see them trot around the garden, and start playing with them. I was impatient to show them my hiding places and secret spots, teach them to climb on the wisteria, and spot bugs in the hedges!

One morning, I woke up from a slightly longer sleep than usual to the sound of Mum calling me.

"Freddy, Freddy! They are here! They're coming!"

I dashed out, expecting to see a procession of black kittens following my Maman. But what I saw was only one. Playful but also fearful, he followed Maman, hiding behind one azalea bush and then the next, jumping over the small ones, dancing around them.

I was about to exclaim, "Only one!" when I saw Maman stop, look behind her, and call as she had called us when she'd wanted us to follow her. I knew then that there were others.

Soon another little head appeared, and then another, even shyer. It took a lot of patience and soft calling for Maman to bring in the fourth and last kitten, the most reticent of them all. Maman led them to the terrace to introduce them. Mum quickly ran into the kitchen to fetch special biscuits for the kittens.

They weren't the hundred I'd hoped for, but four is a nice number. And they were all black! I greeted each of them with a nose touch and a head rub. After snacking, Maman led them to a sunny spot near the bamboo hedge and instructed them to wait there. I heard her talking to them: "Stay here, darlings, your big brother Freddy will look after you. Your Maman has some shopping to do." And then she ran away.

Can you imagine how proud I was? So happy! It was the first time that my Maman needed me! And although she didn't speak to me directly, it was the same. I was in charge! I was needed- my Maman had allowed me to help her, hurray!

The Daltons

At first, my black siblings were so alike that Mum couldn't tell the difference between them. She called them the four Daltons. A few days later, we learned their names: Joey and Lulu for the two boys and Fifi and Maeva for the girls. Joey had almond-shaped eyes and a tiny white spot under his chin. Lulu was the biggest one, with a large round head, and being an incorrigible gourmand, he was a bit fat. Maeva was the cutest kitten ever, and Fifi was very tiny, very shy. My Maman would bring them into the garden every morning, share breakfast with them, and then lead the little band to the usual sunny spot at the bamboo hedge before running away. She knew they were safe under my guard. She usually came back at the end of the afternoon to collect her babies.

She was probably happy to be free again during the day. According to Mum, poor Maman was so young, not more than a year old, and she'd already had two litters! Mum said it was urgent to act soon as the Daltons would grow up. I didn't know what "act" meant, but I understood that it would ease my Maman's life, whatever it was.

FIFI, JOEY AND LULU

Happy Times

When my black brothers and sisters arrived, I started having the best time ever! They were terrific playmates! Joey instantly became my best pal; he was like me, a great explorer and an intrepid adventurer. Often, we'd leave the "little ones" (as we called the others) and escape from the garden for a few hours. Once, we went away for a whole night, and both Mum and Maman were very worried. But we came back, only too happy to be home again. To tell the truth, we have been a bit lost.

Mum didn't tell me that she'd put out an advertisement. She thought it would make me sad. And she was right; I wouldn't like it: she was trying to find new homes for the Daltons.

She took several photos of the four kittens. Then she went around the shops in our shopping street and asked the owners to post her advert: "Four little goblins, the cutest kittens in the world, are looking for loving homes to take them in." Of course, the colour photos were beautiful, so she had several phone calls.

"*Bonjour madame*, what colour are the kittens?" Mum found this kind of question a bit silly. The four kittens were black – this was clear from the photos.

"Oh, black? Oh no! And you don't have any other colour?" Just as if they were selecting a handbag and not a living being with feelings! After the fifth such call, Mum, very annoyed, went round to the shops and removed her ads.

"We like black kitties," she said when she got home. "My little ones, you'll be staying here with Freddy."

Thus, Fifi, Lulu, and Joey stayed with us to my greatest joy. As for Maeva, one of the neighbours fell in love with her, and she went to live with them, not far from our house. We often get news about her. She lives a happy life, watching the hedges in her garden and talking to the birdies, spoilt as only a cat can be.

After a month, Maman stopped coming to collect her babies in the evening, and they were allowed to stay with us. My black siblings didn't mind. They like being with me in the garden or in the house. But they aren't like me. They come inside only on freezing days or when the Yellow Monster from the sky strikes as they don't like it either. It's clearly in the genes! Fifi seemed to enjoy the house at first and spent some time inside, but after a few weeks, she changed her mind and moved back to her basket on the terrace next to her brother Lulu. Joey is different; he is seldom home. He's constantly patrolling the area, coming home only to get food or play with me. Mum worries about him a lot and sometimes calls him until late into the night. But he is so cute! Whenever he comes home, we kiss, rub heads and jump over one another. We're always just so happy to be together again!

Mum learnt through the grapevine that our Maman comes from a generation of stray, half-wild black cats who live in the surrounding area, all refusing to live in a good home like me.

I'll let Mum tell you what happened next with my Maman as these events deeply touched her.

Free as a bird

I noticed that Freddy's Maman had suddenly changed her habits. By the way, I named her Crunchy because, unlike with softer food, she seemed to take time with cat biscuits, chewing them very slowly, sometimes for hours. Anyhow, Crunchy had started coming to dinner and eating quickly before running off again without bothering to check on the kittens. She didn't even glance at them. Only little Fifi would try to follow her but would give up as soon as her Maman jumped over the hedge and disappeared into the next yard. The boys didn't care; they were just too happy in the garden!

I thought it would be the right time to take Crunchy to the vet before another litter of kittens is on the way. But how? She never allowed me to cuddle or even touch her. She would pretend she wanted to claw at my slightest move and then run away. I asked the local cat association for help – they know how to trap street cats. They came, gave me a thousand pieces of advice, and lent me a trap/carrier.

I installed the thing in the garden in the hope it would work. Over the next month, I managed to trap: several hedgehogs, my two usual garden guests, Griset and Big Head; a young fox; the neighbour's beautiful Chartreux; a fierce Norwegian cat, and two street cats that I didn't know. The latter two were taken to the cat association, which found them homes. At least my efforts were not in vain. But my little black Maman, my Crunchy, never came back. I never saw her in the garden, and after a month, I gave up and removed the carrier.

Besides, I had the feeling that this would happen. The day before putting the trap in the garden, I saw Crunchy arriving to claim her lunch. Seeing her through the window, I ran out with a plate of chicken and ham – her favourite foods. I had made it specifically for her. Usually, she would gobble up everything on the plate within minutes. Still, that day, she took only a few tiny bites and walked away.

Astonished, I called out to her: "Crunchy, where are you going? What's wrong?"

I can still see her as clearly as if it had happened just yesterday. She was walking down the small paved alley, leaving. At my call, she stopped, turned, and looked at me for a long time, silent. It was obvious that she wanted to tell me something. I hoped she would come back but she didn't –she resumed walking.

I knew it was a farewell, a goodbye, and thank you for everything.

No matter how many times I waited for her, called her, and looked for her in the area during the following months, I couldn't find her. Later that year, I saw her not far from her first home – the vacant lot where Freddy and Caramel were born. It was no longer a vacant lot but a private property with a house on it. She was crossing the street, heading towards the park. I called to her; she stopped, gave me that same long look, and then ran away as soon as I tried to approach her. That was our last encounter, and it touched me deeply. Crunchy, my little black Maman, was in some way my kitty. I had saved her life; I had saved her first babies and adopted her two litters. I loved her with all my heart, I will never stop loving her...

But we had conflicting aspirations: I wanted to "save" her while she tried to be as free as a bird, even if it meant starving and being cold from time to time. Nevertheless, by going away, she touched me deeply.

A cat behaviour specialist once told me that a cat never stays where she has put her kittens. It's to give them room. Crunchy was probably happy, knowing that her kittens will be taken care of and she went away to find another home for herself.

My Mum is Well

Freddy here, dear reader. Even if Mum doesn't know where our Maman is, I know. Do you remember our relative, auntie Rosalie, from my first story? She has a vast property right in the park. My Maman moved in, and although they aren't the best friends in the world, they get along well together, occasionally quarrelling and sharing tea and biscuits. I escape to the park and pop in to say hello whenever I can. I'm never welcome, though – all I get is a "Little rascal, go back home immediately!"

But I'm sure Maman is happy to see me again!

By the way, my sister Fifi also left our garden one day. She disappeared in the middle of a sunny summer day. For months, Mum searched for her, put up adverts, and placed phone calls to associations and the vets in the area – but no one had seen her.

My Sister's Disappearance

Nobody knows exactly when my sister Fifi left the garden.

The day before it happened, she played with a little blue mouse I had given her. I saw her jumping around and carrying the toy in her mouth from one spot to another. It made me so happy because she didn't have a lot of playthings. Of course, she was free to come into the house and play with any toy we have; she could even take some out to the garden. But she was like her brothers Joey and Lulu. Somehow our Maman had instilled in them the idea that enclosed spaces were dangerous and that it was safer to live outside, free as a bird.

Well, Maman only half succeeded as they rarely left the garden, and if they did, it was only to cross the fence, ready to come back whenever Mum called.

But in winter, or if the weather was cold and rainy, they gladly came inside – although no further than the hallway, where cosy baskets always awaited them. The few times I saw them in the living room was because the Big Yellow Monster, the one that sometimes storms and rages in the sky, was thundering again. When this happened, they would go and sit on the sofa, huddled together like three little chickens, and I would then squeeze between them. They were my Maman's second litter, born shortly after Caramel and me. I love them as if they were my real brothers and sisters.

On this particular day, I saw Fifi again late in the evening. She eventually came running after Mum had almost given up calling her for dinner. It was close to midnight, and it was the third or fourth time (I'm not very good with numbers) that Mum had gone to look for her in the garden. Strange, I thought, she usually arrived as soon as she heard Mum calling her name.

FIFI

It was always so cute watching her arrival! We could hear her before we saw her. Mrrr, mrrr, she would sing somewhere in the neighbour's garden before emerging from the bamboo stems. Mrrr, mew, she would continue singing while crossing the lawn with little jumps. She would join Mum on the terrace and rub her head against her legs to celebrate the "home-coming". Well, the fence crossing, actually. There was much merrymaking each time, and it didn't matter if she had been away for half an hour or had only been ten metres away. Her arrival made me smile each time I saw her.

That evening, however, I wasn't as happy as usual. A feeling of insecurity washed over me and overshadowed my thoughts. I couldn't quite understand it, but it was there.

Gone

The following day when I went out to play, I only saw Lulu and Joey enjoying their breakfast. Fifi was nowhere to be seen.

At first, I didn't care; she may have gone for a walk – she never really went far away. We then became busy playing hide-and-seek and catch-me-if-you-can. You know how it is; time goes by so fast. It was only around lunchtime that I realised she was missing when Mum brought us food.

"Kids, have you seen Fifi this morning?" she asked and called her name several times. We, of course, helped with the calling by meowing very loudly.

"Eat your lunch," said Mum, afraid we would scare Fifi with our boisterous calling. "She'll show up for dinner," she added and went inside.

I knew she wouldn't. I sensed it. But everyone around me looked so confident that I thought I might be wrong. Later in the afternoon, I noticed the blue toy mouse I had given her in the alley. It was lying there, forgotten, destroyed, dirty, and probably untouched since the previous day. The sight of it made me sad. I was sure now: something had happened to Fifi.

She didn't return to the garden that evening, and she didn't answer Mum's calls. No matter how hard I listened, I couldn't hear her little "mrrr, mew" anywhere. I don't remember how many times Mum went into the garden, but it was many. She kept calling Fifi until late into the night. I, too, offered my help; I wanted to go on patrol and look for her. But when I reached the fence, Mum caught me and carried me back into the house.

"Don't worry, Freddy," she said, "she'll be back tomorrow. You know what? We will leave all those cat biscuits on the table outside. I'm sure she'll come to eat later."

That night, as I slept in the bed next to Mum, I noticed her getting up several times, opening the window and calling out, "Fifi! Fifi! Your dinner, darling! Come to eat!"

Freddy's Magic Garden

I leapt up and ran outside as soon as Mum opened the door in the morning. The bowl of biscuits was empty, but I knew that anyone could have eaten them. We have a lot of night visitors, and our gourmet neighbour, the fox from the park, comes often. Sometimes he even tries to take the bowl away because he thinks it will magically fill itself, like in one of my previous stories, "The House on the Corner". Unable to keep it in his mouth while jumping over the fence, the fox inevitably drops it.

I started searching in the garden first, with Joey and Lulu. We explored the thick bamboo hedge, and I climbed inside the wisteria – in summer, it has so many branches and leaves that it could be the perfect hiding place. I often use it to trick Big Head, and he never finds me.

But despite our meticulous inspection, we couldn't find Fifi anywhere.

"Let's go on patrol," I suggested.

"Yes, yes, let's go!" shouted Joey. He is an intrepid explorer, always ready for an adventure, and some-times ventures so far from home that he gets lost. But he always finds his way back, eventually. In contrast, Lulu wasn't very keen come. He seldom leaves the garden because he's always concerned Mum may

199

serve some good food while he's away. Such a big gourmet, our Lulu! Nevertheless, he agreed to come with us, and we left.

First, we searched in the surrounding gardens. Our three garden pals joined the mission: we met Griset, who offered to help; we met Mozart, who also came with us. Then we met Satine, who asked if by chance we'd taken some provisions with us, in which case she would gladly carry them.

"To eat them, you mean?" asked Lulu, guessing her intention.

We also met Spot and Spectre. And some kitties we didn't know, and everyone offered to help. Ah, and sister Pearl also came running after us from our garden. She was a bit annoyed as we hadn't asked her to come, but she was also excited to participate in something she thought was a game.

But it wasn't a game. By the end of the day, there were 12 of us searching for Fifi. Maybe we were more, but that's as far as I can count. We patrolled farther than we ever had, observing everything, inspecting all the hedges along our way.

We found no trace of Fifi, not even a tuft of fur, not even a footprint that could have belonged to her. She had vanished. She didn't come to dinner that day, the next day, or the day after. A whole week passed, and there was not even the slightest trace of her, no indication that she had ever put a paw in the garden again.

Mum didn't lose faith. Several times a day, she would go outside and call for Fifi. In the evenings, she didn't hesitate to stay out until late into the night, searching everywhere, looking for her, exploring the neighbourhood. At night, she doubled the portion of food she used to leave outside "so there will be enough for Fifi if she returns".

She kept telling us that Fifi would show up sooner or later, but I believe it may have been more to comfort herself than us. She also asked us to stay next to the house and stop our patrols for a while. I wonder why Mum didn't appreciate our help; exploring the neighbourhood was very useful! She should have been a bit more grateful, right? Anyway, I carried the blue mouse into the bamboo hedge next to the fence. Maybe Fifi would come back for it and take it with her. If I were ever to leave home, I'd take my little green teddy bear with me so I wouldn't feel alone.

After a week of unsuccessful waiting, calling, and searching, we saw Mum leave the house with many leaflets and glue. Soon, we would see Fifi's picture posted wherever we went: on the electricity poles, in the shop windows, on the trees, on the fences of the houses around, on the mailboxes.

I could read a little and I could decipher the first word, written with big letters: "LOST", and underneath was a picture of Fifi. In my opinion, this is not the way to do it. Imagine Fifi walking past the poster and reading "LOST" above her picture. She would think that Mum had lost her photo! She would probably think, "Oh, not a big deal! Mum certainly has plenty more!" and walk further. No, Mum should have written, "Come home, Fifi!" And she should have added: "We promise that Charlotte will never show up again."

You see, if Fifi had disappeared, it was because of Charlotte.

Charlotte

A few weeks before Fifi left the garden, something happened.

It was very late when Mum arrived home holding a small cat in her arms one night. "I saved her by the skin of her teeth," she told us. "A truck had been about to run over her. I stopped it in the nick of time. You know, my little ones, I almost had to pull her out from under the huge wheels. This little girl was running like crazy from left to right in the middle of the street. Don't ever do that, my sweeties!"

She put the cat down among us. She was a calico girl, a beauty. I thought I would give her a kiss, but luckily, I didn't. This furious little thing could well have bitten me! She started to spit and growl at us, and she even slapped Cannelle! So Mum took her into another room and offered her food and water. We watched through the glass door – she was so hungry! She devoured several bowls of cat biscuits in one go, then made herself cosy in a basket as if she had always been part of the family. And she started to nap. Boy! Was she thinking of settling with us?

"She must be exhausted, poor thing," said Mum, carefully closing the door after her as she came out. She asked us to be quiet.

The following day, Mum took her to the vet. The kitty had no identification, and the vet had never seen her before. Mum was sure that the little girl lived somewhere in the neighbourhood. With the cat in her arms, she went to look at all the houses around us. I went with her. You can imagine, this was too much fun. We, I mean, Mum, rang the door-bells of the houses. Humans came out, talked to Mum, and some even petted the calico girl and me. But they all said they didn't know her. Eventually, we arrived at a small, old house, five or seven homes away from ours. A young woman opened the door. Yes, it was their cat, she said.

But strangely enough, Charlotte – as she called her – didn't want to leave Mum's arms. She didn't want to go back home. I could see it, and I could feel it, too. I knew something was wrong. Besides, why had she been so hungry the night before? She had a home; she wasn't a stray.

To lure her in, the woman brought her "food": four tiny cat biscuits on a plate! My! Not even enough for a bite! Was this all the poor girl was getting at home? I felt sorry for Charlotte. I wished Mum would take her back to our house; I was even sad when I saw her handing the kitty over to this person!

I shouldn't have been. The very next day, Charlotte appeared in our garden again. As soon as Mum opened the front door, she stepped into the house. Without a second thought, she strode into the kitchen, finished all the leftovers, and, having selected a sunny spot on the terrace, decided to stay. In the evening, Mum took her back to her house. "Charlotte wants to move in," said Mum to us.

It lasted for a while: every morning, the calico kitty would arrive at our house, eat whatever she found and ask for more, then stay in the garden to nap. Mum would take her back to her house each evening – except on the weekends. On the weekends, there was nobody to answer the door at Charlotte's home. Her people used to go away on Friday night and only return on Monday morning. What happened to their cat was the least of their worries. The story repeated for a couple of weeks – and the little calico kitty ended up spending almost all her time with us. We didn't mind. We gradually got used to her, and she to us, and it was even fun having her in the garden.

However, I noticed several times how mean she was to Fifi. She would lash out at her whenever she saw her. My poor sister only dared to come into the garden at night when Charlotte was either back at her home or sleeping in our house.

I wrongly thought that Fifi would step up sooner or later, declare this was her home and draw the lines. I had not imagined that the one to give up would be Fifi.

Thus, one sunny afternoon in July, she decided to leave the garden. That same day, I saw her playing with the blue mouse I had given her, so happy, so joyful! I felt so pleased watching her funny game.

Little did I know that I would not see her again for a long time.

A Very Long Absence

Mum says that losing someone you love is terrible but that eventually, the pain fades away little by little. But when you lose someone and don't know what happened to your loved one, the pain is not only double - it's everlasting. I know something about that. How much I suffered during those few days when I couldn't find my Maman and sister Caramel and didn't know what had happened to them!

The feeling was the same, this time. Mum and I were so worried about Fifi! Mum continued to look around. She would often leave for the whole day with even more flyers. I didn't check, but I'm sure the three surrounding towns were covered with pictures of Fifi. She had become a celebrity. Every cat association, every shelter, and vet for miles around had her photo and ID number.

"Someone will find her one day and bring her back to us; you'll see, my little ones," Mum told us, totally exhausted whenever she returned from her investigations. I wasn't sure whether to believe her. However, I kept looking for her, with the help of my garden friends. Joey, Lulu, Mozart, Griset, and I continued to patrol everywhere. We even signed a truce with Big Head, a temporary non-aggression treaty. He's the only one who dares to venture to the centre of Paris. Perhaps Fifi had gone shopping and forgotten to come back. The windows of Parisian shops can be so tempting!

As for the Maine Coons, they couldn't help with the search in the garden as they were only allowed to go onto the patio. Nevertheless, they could see a large portion of the hedge, so they did help with the watching. Daddy cat Uddy also organised recitals each evening at 6 pm exactly. He would gather all his kids on the bench in the corner and give the signal. Then you could hear seven Maine Coons howling and yowling even if you were a distance away. The effort was noteworthy, even if it was not harmonious, given that daddy Uddy sings totally out of tune. Don't tell him I said this, though. Poor guy, he's so proud of his voice! He often sings one of his hits at three or four in the morning, dedicated to Mum.

Anyway, it didn't attract Fifi.

A month passed, then two, then three, then six months. Then a year and yet another one. After the third year, I think even Mum had lost hope of finding

Fifi again. I feel so, although I'm not sure; Mum always believes everything is possible.

Then One Day. . .

I remember it very well: it was a Friday afternoon in winter. The festivities were barely over, and the Christmas decorations had not yet been put away. The telephone rang. Mum picked it up, listened, and then exclaimed, "Fifi!"

We quickly gathered around her. "Meow, meow, meow! Did they find her? Where is she? How is she?" We wanted to know everything all at once.

Mum hurriedly put on her coat and trainers.

"I'm going to fetch her," she said. "She's at a vet in the next town. I won't be long."

I wanted to go with her, but she told me to wait at home. Fifi was well, she said; she would be back very soon.

Indeed, Mum brought a black kitty home in the carrier not even an hour later. We all went to smell her, each of us wanting to check that it was our Fifi and not another black cat. Of course, the ID matched, but that wasn't enough proof for us. Nothing replaces a smell; it's our way of identifying everything, and it's far more reliable than other means.

We soon realised that there was no doubt – our sister had come back! It was her, our beloved little Fifi. She recognised us immediately, and the reunion was full of headbutts, nose kisses and purring. Nobody would have laughed if you had said you thought the living room had become an airport runaway full of planes ready to take off. Such was the noise from all the purring.

Mum later told us that as soon as she stepped into the vet's office, Fifi had started purring.

Where Had She Been?

Where she had been for three years remains a mystery. Mum only managed to retrace the last four months of Fifi's adventure. The person who had taken her to the vet was a cat shelter member. An old lady in the neighbouring town called her for help. A starving little black cat appeared at her house one day. She started to feed her, and the kitty had settled in her garden. She never entered the house, and they were both happy, the kitty and the lady. I hope that she had at least arranged a cosy basket under a shelter for my sister. But we don't know. Maybe I should go there one day and investigate.

Then one day, the old lady noticed that the kitty's fur had become dull and lost its pretty sheen, and she had a spot on her back. She supposed the cat had a health problem. She did not want to care for a sick cat, so she called that cat shelter person who took Fifi to the vet. It's there that, during the exam, the vet found the kitty was chipped.

Mum took Fifi to our vet the same week she had brought her home. She did have a tooth problem, but everything was back to normal after minor surgery. She's now in perfect health and so happy to be home!

So, we know what happened to her during the last four months of her odyssey. But before that? For more than three years? Where had she been?

Her character has changed. Whereas she had never wanted to stay in, now Fifi never asks to go out. The house has become her haven. Soon after arriving home, she tested all the baskets, beds, sofas, and cushions and decided that they belonged to her, all of them. She eats non-stop and always asks for something better, some extra food, such as chicken or fresh fish. Mum grooms her as much as possible, and nothing is too good for her. She is also very much afraid of strangers. If a visitor arrives, Fifi hides under the bed and stays hidden long after the person has left.

Did someone perhaps find her wandering the streets and take her to another city where she got lost? Was she living in a house, unable to escape at first but then ran away and ended up in the old lady's garden? Mum found out the old lady's house looked a bit like ours. We'll never know. Mum assumes that she first wandered from garden to garden, from place to place and that, at least in the early days, she must have wanted to go back home. But she must have been chased away by the fierce Charlotte.

Now, she has nothing to fear. Charlotte's family moved away and took their cat with them. We asked to keep Charlotte, to adopt her, but they refused. We hope she's well.

We are all so happy that Fifi is with us again! I allow her to borrow my toys (well, not all), and we play together every night until the early morning hours. I'm not sure whether Mum appreciates it, but she's so happy to have Fifi home! She says that seeing Fifi every morning when she wakes up is like a miracle repeating itself day after day.

The Kitty with Nine Lives

I t all started one Friday afternoon.

We were alone at home. Well, not quite. Laura, the cleaning lady, was there to look after us.

When her work day was over, she made us all come inside. Mum doesn't want us to be outside when she's not home. I break that rule a lot because I'm not worried about anything. I have been through so much in my life already that there is nothing I'm afraid of. What, Mum? Oh yes, except the Yellow Monster! But let's forget it for a while, the time I tell you this story.

That evening, I had been asleep on the patio and was surprised. So, I went inside with the others. Well, by mistake.

Once Laura thought we were all safe, she closed the windows and doors, put the shutters down, grabbed her handbag and left.

She didn't count us, as Mum usually does, to make sure no one was missing. A mistake that led to dramatic consequences.

We went upstairs to the kitchen to get something to eat – there is always plenty of cat biscuits available in our house because Mum is afraid we will "starve". And we pretend to starve quite often – every time there's the aroma of chicken or fish coming from the kitchen!

After having a snack, each of us found his or her favourite basket for a little nap while waiting for Mum. She was particularly late that evening; we had to wait for hours. Finally, we heard the sound of the key in the lock. Mum! We all jumped up and ran to the front door. We welcomed her with joy and excitement and also with some annoyance! The "where have you been all day" and "why are you so late" questions were purring in from all sides. Daddy cat demanded a special dinner as compensation – he ordered treats, tuna, ham, fish and more treats. We all agreed, but some of us refused to eat because the dishes served did not wholly meet our expectations. Ah, the service is getting worse in our kitchen!

Nobody noticed that Valentina wasn't with us with all that excitement and turmoil. She never eats any food other than cat biscuits.

After filling our tummies, we ran to Mum's bedroom and jumped on her bed, as we usually do when it's time to sleep. We stretched all over the place, made ourselves comfortable and started calling for Mum in a somewhat impetuous way. Was she finally going to join us? What was she doing now? Finally, she entered the bedroom and it was time for cuddles, our favourite moment of the day. We purred and purred and rubbed our heads against Mum's hands, curled around her, and fell asleep.

But not for long. Suddenly, Mum woke up and hurried out of the bedroom. Naturally, we followed her.

Mum is in the best position to tell you what happened next.

Suddenly, something woke me up. Yet there was no noise, on the contrary. A profound silence reigned in the house, a heavy, uneasy, somehow distressing silence. What was it? I had never felt this before. Instinctively, I began to count the cats. They were all around me.

Except for Valentina.

I realised that I hadn't seen her since I got home. I started looking for her, calling her name. The kitties helped and followed me from one room to another. We searched everywhere – in all the places she fancied, but also under the bed, in the dressing room, in the places she never used to go, and even in the spots where there wasn't room for a cat. We looked in the most unlikely spots and opened all the cupboards and drawers, hoping to find her curled up in a deep sleep each time. Yet she wasn't anywhere. After an hour of thorough searching, it became clear: she wasn't in the house.

I put on my slippers and dressing gown and went into the garden with a torch. I carefully closed the front door behind me to not have to look for eight cats simultaneously; one was more than enough.

I checked every bush three times. I parted all the branches, went around the house five times, and looked over the fences in case she was in a neighbour's garden. I upended every single object that happened to be in my way. I called her, my voice growing louder and louder as if this would bring her back. An annoyed neighbour opened his window and asked for peace. A dog barked nearby to endorse the man's words. If Valentina were close by, that noise would only have scared her more. I went back into the house and again searched hopelessly here and there. Not knowing what to do, I sent a message to my son. He was in London. Despite the late hour, he replied immediately.

"Don't worry! She must be sleeping somewhere. She will appear again in the morning."

Maybe he was right. Maybe she was hidden in some unlikely place. Or perhaps, she was outside and would be waiting for me at the front door in the morning. It was the middle of the night, and there was nothing else I could do until the morning.

Valentina isn't allowed to wander freely in the garden; she doesn't know how to behave in open spaces. When outside, she becomes scared, runs in all directions, and desperately calls for help. It was all the more worrying not to find or even hear her. She is a highly vulnerable and sensitive cat. I knew she would feel helpless, lost, and alone outside.

When we moved from the small flat to our big house, I first noticed how emotional she is. To keep the kitties safe while the movers went to and fro, I closed all the cats in one room in the flat. My idea was to take them to the house when all the furniture was moved, and the movers had left. But the whole process lasted far longer than expected. It was very late when I went back to fetch the kitties. They were all fine – except Valentina. Her eyes were full of tears; she ran to me and hid in my lap. Some would say that cats don't cry. But they do. At least Valentina does. She knew that she would have to leave her beloved birthplace and sadness had overwhelmed her.

Once in the new house, she stayed under my bed for the first three days. She needed three weeks to look through my bedroom's half-open door and another two months to put just one paw on the patio. Meanwhile, her dad Uddy and her sister Vanille had explored the house from top to bottom the minute they got inside!

I was up again before sunrise, firmly believing that she'd be waiting for me at the front door. I ran down first thing to check and was both discouraged and distraught. She wasn't in the garden either. I went back into the house, dressed, had a coffee, and went out looking for my kitty.

I felt she must be around somewhere. A shy cat never strays far from home. I searched the street, looked under parked cars, and shouted her name in the sewer shafts in case she had taken refuge in one of them. A neighbour's cat had once lurked in a sewer shaft near her house for seven days without anyone guessing she was there.

I looked over the hedges into my neighbours' gardens. Some of them came out of their houses and joined me in the search. After an hour, seven of us tried to find my Valentina. But to no avail.

Later that morning, I made posters with her picture, her name, her little name, and my phone number, and then went to put them up wherever possible. The whole quarter was decorated with her beautiful face. People stopped, looked at the poster, and exclaimed, "What a beautiful kitty!" but no one had seen her. I called all the vets in the area – if anyone brought in a beautiful tabby Maine Coon, could they call me? She was microchipped.

The search continued into the afternoon. A caretaker from the building across the street came to help, and his arrival gave me an idea. Could she have run into the underground garage of their building? We went to look. The garage was closed by the heavy automatic door, and the parking places inside were the lock-ups, mostly closed. Thus it was impossible to hide in. However, I noticed a strange shape on the high ceiling – a kind of pipe made of concrete that ran its length. It seemed plain, but could it be that there were some openings, some connections leading from the outside into the lock-ups? By chance, one of them was standing open, so we looked up from inside, and indeed, there was a small opening. The caretaker said that the pipe itself was divided into several compartments.

"Where does it lead to?" I asked. "Is it connected to the outside?"

"Nowhere," he replied. "It does not extend to the outside." He was sure about this.

That day and in the days that followed, I spent all my free time looking for Valentina. I neglected everything – my work, my cats. I even forgot to eat most of the time. So-called "well-intentioned" people started telling me I would never find her. I didn't mind, I knew it: my kitty was waiting for me to come and take her home. She trusted me. She was sure I would come, so I had to find her, undoubtedly.

On the sixth day, I resolved to enlarge my search area to the park and walked towards it. But halfway through, I turned around and walked back. All of a sudden, I knew where she was. It was as if someone had suddenly given me the answer to a riddle; as if my kitty had sent me a message: "Here I am; you walked by but didn't see me. Come back, Mum; I'm waiting for you!"

I was so sure of my intuition that I almost ran – directly to the caretaker of the building opposite our house.

"I know where she is!" I exclaimed excitedly, out of breath, "She is inside the concrete pipe in your garage. Who is the owner of the first lock-up?"

I think he believed I had lost my mind. How could a cat enter the garage, find an open lock-up, jump up four-meter-high to the ceiling, and slip into the concrete pipe? Provided there was a hole to get in - we found out those openings in the concrete were irregular and didn't exist for all lock-ups. And why was I asking him about the first lock-up specifically? I couldn't explain. I was sure of one thing: my kitty was there, waiting for me, and I had to get her out. It was becoming urgent. Stuck inside a narrow dark space from the first day (which I supposed), she wouldn't have been able to get out again, wouldn't have had anything to eat for six days, and wouldn't have had access to water.

The caretaker stated again that there were no connections linking the garage ceiling to the garden. As I insisted, he promised to find out who owned the first lock-up and call me back.

And he did it that same evening. The news wasn't good: the owners were in Japan and weren't due back before a week. One week more in that narrow dark space? This would mean a fortnight for my kitty – far too long to survive without food and water.

"But they must have left you their mobile phone number?"

No, he said, he didn't have their mobile, but he had the phone number of their son, a doctor in a Parisian hospital. He called him but couldn't reach him that evening. He promised to try the following day again.

I couldn't sleep that night; I was so confident that Valentina would be home again the very next day.

However, there were still many challenges to overcome. Once informed of our request, the doctor agreed to call his parents in Japan and ask where he could find a key to the lock-up. Had they taken it with them on their trip? No, the key was in their flat.

After performing surgery at his hospital, the kind man managed to find the time to rush to his parent's flat. He retrieved the key and brought it to the caretaker, happy that he could help.

Thus, on the seventh day after Valentina's escape, the key became available at the end of the afternoon.

Hi, it's me again, Freddy!

We should be forever grateful to this caretaker, said Mum, so I went purring in gratitude to his office as soon as the following day. Indeed, to our greatest joy, that evening, we saw Mum coming back with Valentina! But oh, she was in deplorable shape. Curled in Mum's arms, she was covered with dead leaves and dirt, her eyes were closed, and she could hardly breathe. We helped Mum take care of her, comforting her by gathering around and purring loudly.

That same evening, Mum told us what had happened. It was quite an adventure! Of course, I was happy but also a bit annoyed: she should have taken me with her because I could certainly have helped.

Mum, you better take over from here.

* * *

When we opened the lock-up, we couldn't see any sign of the cat. The owner's car was parked inside, its doors closed. We looked on top of the car, under it, and inspected all the corners of the small space twice, but Valentina wasn't there. I looked up. Indeed, as I had guessed, and because it was the starting point of the concrete pipe, there was a rather small hole, which at least would allow us to look inside. The caretaker went home to fetch a ladder as the ceiling was very high. He came back with one – and also with his father-in-law, who had offered to help.

The caretaker climbed up, and I held my breath. At first, he couldn't see anything. Then, after lighting up the concrete pipe with his phone, he exclaimed: "I see a shape! What colour is your cat?"

"Beige-brown," I said. Frankly, I wasn't even a little surprised. Despite everyone telling me it was impossible, I knew she was there.

But the hole was narrow, and the pipe itself wasn't large. Nevertheless, the brave caretaker – a very slim and tall man – managed to slip inside. Seeing him disappear into the hole, I became afraid for him: he could get stuck at any moment! I would have preferred to call the firefighters. But he was already inside the narrow space. Wouldn't Valentina be frightened by him and retreat further into the depths of the thin pipe? She would then be totally out of reach. But she didn't. She wisely waited to be fetched. I firmly believe she knew then it was her last chance to get out, last chance to survive. Soon, the caretaker called from above: "I've got her! I'm holding her!"

I think those were the sweetest words I had ever heard.

"Help me get out of here!" he asked, and his father-in-law went up the ladder to fetch him. He pulled out the caretaker with my cat in his arms.

They were both safe. What extraordinary courage this man had!

I didn't take Valentina to the vet that evening. It was late, and the local vets were already closed. I could have taken her to our usual clinic, which is open days and nights, but this would have meant hours of waiting as their waiting room was always over-crowded. Considering it better for the kitty to wait the following morning, I cleaned her coat and eyes – almost entirely closed by tears and dirt. I tried to feed her, but she wouldn't accept water or food. Using an eyedropper, I managed to get her to drink a few drops, then wrapped her in a soft blanket and let her rest. Nothing appeared to be broken, but her breathing worried me – it was uneven. I thought it was perhaps just the emotion and that she would be better the next day.

But she wasn't. The local vet agreed to see her urgently. And it was then when I thought she was safe, that the bad news came.

After several exams, the vet found out she had a small wound on one of her lungs, probably caused by a violent fall. This had triggered pleural effusion, and because she hadn't been treated for the injury for many days, a lot of fluid had accumulated in her lungs. Her chest was filled with liquid, compressing her lungs and impeding normal breathing.

The vet, a woman, said there was nothing she could do about it. The cat was bound to suffocate sooner or later. Any interventions were impossible as she would not survive the anaesthesia. Did I want her to be put down so that she would not suffer any longer?

"What do you mean to put down?" I replied. "I have just found her, and now I will have to lose her again? No way!"

I installed Valentina in her carrier and set off to our famous clinic, where we go any time one of our cats has a major problem. Founded in the 19th century, it is the best animal care hospital in the country.

The traffic was heavy that day, and my kitty's condition was rapidly deteriorating. Once at the clinic and before going into the waiting room, I took the time to check her state. My poor darling looked at me, her eyes full of tears. She put her paws on my hand and still found the strength to purr. "Save me, please, Mum," she was telling me with her beautiful look. I felt so helpless! Losing my usual courage, I thought that the end had come . .

The big waiting room was full of pet owners. It would take at least three hours to see a vet, said the young woman at the reception desk. Three hours? Valentina couldn't wait that long; her lifespan was no longer counted in hours but in minutes. With a trembling voice, I asked if we could be admitted immediately. I don't know how I looked, but the woman immediately called a vet after just glancing at me. Probably my face expressed total despair. A doctor arrived, took the carrier without a word, and disappeared.

I waited for a long time in the waiting room, between the dogs and cats, some of which were running around happily, playing with one another. I wish you could have seen them, my babies, you who are always so afraid of visiting the vet! Some kitties and dogs like it. They even make friends in the waiting room!

Finally, the vet called me in. She confirmed the diagnosis I'd already heard from my local vet.

"We can try a live puncture without anaesthetic," she said. This was the only hope, with a three to five per cent chance of survival, according to her. It was a hazardous procedure given the cat's condition. Anaesthesia was out of the question; she would never wake up again.

The decision was up to me. I left her office to get some fresh air in their little courtyard. Again, I called my son.

"Let her go in peace," he advised.

Back to the vet's office, I asked her to go ahead with the puncture. A three to five per cent chance of survival, I thought, is far better than zero. Didn't she survive seven days in a dark hole without food and water? She is a courageous kitty, and I trusted she would make it. Besides, she had never been ill until then.

I asked to see Valentina again to hold her in my arms and kiss her. I told her everything would be fine, and she would be back home soon. I hope she didn't feel that my voice was shaking.

We had agreed that if I didn't receive a phone call from the vet during the next 12 hours, it would mean that all went well.

And the vet didn't call until the following day. I learnt then that they had given Valentina a double puncture without being tranquillised, which she had bravely endured. She had to stay in the clinic for three more days. I thought she had now been saved.

However, when I went to fetch her, the vets weren't optimistic. She still had a tiny wound on her lung, and nothing could be done to stop the pleural effusion permanently. They didn't know how long she would live. The prognosis was unfavourable. It could last a week, three weeks maybe. A month at most.

I didn't react to their prognosis; I was hardly listening. The vets seemed surprised at my total lack of concern. Was I an insensitive woman? Of course not; I just knew that they were wrong. My Valentina had no intention of leaving me any time soon.

Hi, Freddy again. I will take over from here.

When Valentina finally came back home. I asked her to tell us what had happened, but she didn't want to. She said she had forgotten all about it, it didn't count anymore, and was happy to be home again. However, because I'm inquisitive, I went to explore the area around the garage. I found a small hole in the grass, leading somewhere into the dark. It was frightful! Even I, the most courageous cat in the world. . . What, Mum? Well then, one of the most courageous cats, wouldn't dare slip inside.

Unless, of course, the Yellow Monster chased me around. Did Valentina meet him, too? A big yellow dog in the neighbourhood furiously barks at every-thing that moves – maybe he is the yellow monster's employee?

All this happened five years ago, and Valentina is still with us despite an unfavourable prognosis. Mind you, she used several of her nine lives each time she was saved! First, there was this intuition that Mum got. Then, the friendly lock-up owners arranged directly from Japan that their garage space was open. Then, the kind doctor raced across town after performing surgery so that he could get us the key. And finally, the brave caretaker dared enter such an impossible place. Oh, I forgot to mention the two wonderful vets who decided to try the impossible. Valentina can be called a lucky kitty, can't she? So many odds turned out to be in her favour!

But I have warned her to be careful from now on. Despite this, she recently decided to spend another of her life. Ah, she can be extravagant! She fell so seriously ill that Mum called us all around her and asked us to say goodbye to her before taking her to the vet. Again, the prognostic was very dark, and Mum returned home with tears in her eyes, without Valentina.

But you know what? After a day at the clinic, our Valentina was back home! Happy and impassive as always.

How many times have vets predicted the end of her life! "You know", they say to Mum, "she'll only be here for a week or two". And Mum leaves with her kitty, not believing a word. And when she brings Valentina back several months later for some minor problem, the vets wonder: "What? Valentina? She's still around? Unbelievable!"

And Valentina and Mum both smile. Mum is happy to have such a brave, determined fighter cat, and Valentina is delighted to be with us for many more years to come.

VALENTINA

Defying Adversity

A family was going to a holiday resort where cats weren't allowed. But they had a cat. What were they to do? The answer was obvious. After spending a night in a lovely B&B, a large mansion in the countryside, they decided to leave the kitty behind. That's how, one day, at the beginning of July, a tiny tabby kitten found herself alone in the gardens unknown to her. Her family had simply "forgotten" her.

"Cannelle will be fine here, won't she?" asked the woman.

"Of course, it's such a nice place for a cat with all these gardens! And I'm sure someone will adopt her – she's so pretty!" replied the man.

"Yes, and so young, still a little kitten. People like kittens."

So they both agreed.

Only their little girl was sad. She wanted to cry, but her parents promised to get her another kitten when they returned from holiday. "It will be an even more beautiful kitty, you'll see!"

The woman took Cannelle in her arms and placed her behind a large bush not far from the B&B entrance. "*Petite*, we need to leave. You just go and play around," she said in farewell as if she were leaving for a few hours. A slight tap on the kitty's head and the family got into the car. When she tried to join them, they slammed the car door in front of her tiny nose and drove away.

"Yikes!" exclaimed the man. "Phew," breathed the woman in relief, then added, "It's a shame. Poor thing."

The little girl wiped away a tear. Then she thought about that other kitten she would get when they returned from holiday – or maybe a new coloured pencil set?

As for the kitty, she sat there, bewildered. She knew she wouldn't see them again. Why was she being left behind? Did they not love her anymore? Wasn't she their little kitty, the princess of the house? And what should she do now? Run after the car? Dogs do it, but cats are too proud.

"If they don't like me, I don't like them either," decided Cannelle. She was a brave, optimistic little kitten, and deep inside her little heart, she knew something good was waiting for her, somewhere ahead in her life. Soon, she'd get a new mum, and this time they'd stay together forever. It was a certitude; how could it be otherwise?

The Broom the Kick and a Ladle

She looked towards the big mansion. Giant steps lead to the entrance. The door was wide open, and she could smell croissants! *Ah,* thought Cannelle, *that's where the breakfast room for cats is!* She loved croissants.

Bravely, she walked to the B&B and climbed the stairs with some difficulty - they were steep! She strode into the dining room, her tail high in anticipation. What a wonderful place! Leftovers were all around. Something was waiting for her on every table: cheese, slices of ham, and even a full plate of croissants! And there was a large jug of milk, what a delight! No doubt, her breakfast was ready, waiting for her to indulge. And oh, look! There was even a waiter who was busy sweeping. He was undoubtedly waiting for her arrival to attend to her. She had come to the right place!

"Don't bother; I can help myself," cried Cannelle and jumped on a table.

Unfortunately, this waiter wasn't very good with foreign languages – French people seldom are. He heard "meow" but didn't understand what it meant.

"*La peste*!" he shouted and continued with a string of words that should not be repeated in polite company.

He ran towards the kitty with an angry look, his broom lifted in the air, ready to fall on the kitty. Poor man! He didn't know that he was holding a magic broom! A broom that wouldn't want to harm a little kitten for no reason in the world. Instead, it chose to land its powerful blow on an expensive Limoges porcelain set, breaking it into a thousand pieces.

Before the waiter could get over the shock, Cannelle grabbed a piece of croissant between her teeth and ran into the gardens. She hid inside a thick hedge to enjoy her booty. She wouldn't have wanted to stay in the dining room anyway. Really, some people simply have no manners. How rude! A "pest", he'd called her – the cat who was a princess! She had never doubted that she was the descendant of a long line of noble cats, aristo-cats of the highest rank. Besides, all cats are royal, aren't they?

"I won't go back! Too bad for that stupid waiter. Now he won't have anyone to help him with the leftovers," she muttered as she enjoyed her snatched croissant. Of course, it wasn't much, but it made her happy for a while.

It was time to tour the property – her new "home". She sniffed the hedges, raced between the trees, tried to catch a butterfly and rolled over the daisies. When lunchtime arrived, she detected the delicious smell of roast chicken wafting across the gardens.

"Ah, I hope they serve it with fresh pasta and gravy." Cannelle was a true gourmet; she knew how to match dishes. Again, she climbed the big stairs. The smell was so appealing that she was ready to forget the morning's misadventure.

Albeit a little uneasy, she sashayed into the dining room, thus generously providing the waiter with an opportunity to make amends. The least he could do was offer her a nice chicken breast.

But do you think that stupid guy would understand the glorious occasion he had been given? He ran towards her and kicked her little bum as hard as he could! The kick was so powerful that it sent the poor kitten straight into the garden. That was a bit painful! Some guests protested; some were even shocked. The waiter justified himself: "There are dozens of stray cats here. If we feed them all, there will soon be hundreds, thousands! One should never feed a stray cat; they just keep coming back."

Even the guests who disagreed didn't want to argue with him – you don't want to get the worst piece of chicken, do you? Better to agree with this influential character unless you want to be served a three-day-old dish.

As for Cannelle, she sat in the shade of a large tree, licked her little bum and decided to have a nap. Her mummy cat used to say that napping replaces food when there isn't any.

She woke up late in the afternoon feeling very hungry. As often happens in France, the mouth-watering smell of good cuisine floated in the air around her. Where was it coming from? Could there be a cat restaurant somewhere at the back of the mansion? She set out to find it. As she trotted to the rear of the building, she thought about how the Chef must be very famous and licked her chops in anticipation of a delicious meal.

It wasn't difficult to find the kitchen, and what a stroke of luck! The door was wide open, and the place was as busy as an anthill. Tens of men in white were bustling around the stoves, handling pots and pans, cooking, frying, and dishing up food. Waiters came and went, entering through a swinging door, grabbing a plate or two and carrying them away. *What a funny game*, thought Cannelle; *I'll go and help!*

She entered cautiously, her belly to the ground. Have you ever wondered why we cats sometimes crawl this way? Well, it's simple: it makes us invisible!

Once in the kitchen, she jumped on a counter. There were so many dishes in front of her, so many delights! A dream for a hungry kitty. Which one to select?

The most tempting, it seemed to her, was a nice fish fried in butter. *I'll take this one*, thought Cannelle. She seized the fish by the tail, lifted it up, which was no easy task, and began to drag it along the counter. It was about twice her size! The kitchen staff, finally noticing her, started to laugh. Unfortunately, this had the effect of arousing the attention of the Chef.

He stepped out of his tiny office, grabbed the first tool he could find – a big ladle – and ran towards Cannelle. *Ah, here comes help*, thought Cannelle. *But why is he swinging the ladle in the air? And why does he keep shouting?*

"The cat! The thief!" the Chef yelled, his face angry and red. "You idiots didn't see it? And you let the cat come in and steal the food?"

Cannelle looked around her to see which thief he was talking about and couldn't see any.

As the ladle and the man were getting too close to her, she decided it would be wise to leave. Without dropping the fish, she jumped over the dishes and glassware; she heard the sound of pots breaking behind, but that was the least of her worries. Luckily, she escaped just in time – but we cannot say the same for the glassware. A lot of dishes were broken in that B&B.

The kitty ran out into a thick hedge. The fish was no longer whole; however, enough was left for a delectable dinner.

Happy, her belly full for the first time that day, she made a bed of dry leaves, curled up into a ball and fell asleep.

Learning to Survive

Cannelle awoke early the following day, stretched happily, and meowed to claim her breakfast. Then she suddenly remembered that she wasn't in her home anymore, and no one was there to attend to her. She recalled the kick, the ladle and the broom. Phew! What a scary day she'd had!

"I need to do something about the food situation", decided Cannelle and set off to find the venue where the cats' breakfast was served. She had seen a few other cats roaming the gardens – they would certainly know! Two kitties were chatting not far away, and Cannelle decided to engage in a bit of conversation.

"Pardon me," she said politely. "Where is the dining room for cats?"

"Haha," laughed one of them, a big white cat. "Look at that princess! A dining room for cats? And maybe you want your food served on a golden plate?"

The other one, a small tabby kitty, seemed more friendly: "Don't make fun of her; she's new here. Aren't you, my little one?"

"My family left me here yesterday, but they'll be back! They love me!" Cannelle knew they would never come back, but she was too proud to admit it. "You see, I went to the big dining room yesterday, and later I went to the kitchen and. . . ."

"Oh woe, never put your paws in those cursed places!" cried both kitties, and one could sense they had some relevant experience. "It's not the food they give you; it's kicks and pokes!"

"The best you can do is wait until it's completely dark, then go to the bins behind the kitchen. There may be some food scraps to pick up," advised the tabby cat.

But the white one didn't seem happy. "Why are you telling her? There are already enough of us around the bins!"

Cannelle let them argue and went on a scouting trip to find out where this famous Bins restaurant was. Food scraps! A few days ago, she would have turned her back in disdain if someone had mentioned them. But here, they sounded like the promise of a feast.

Making a Friend

She got a bit lost during her search. She wandered into the country beyond the gardens, saw even more cats and met some exotic ones. Boy, how big they were! They were mostly white, but some were brown, had big horns and beards and wore shoes! And look at that, they feasted on grass as if it were the best food in the world! Were they dangerous? Cautiously, she approached one of them, a little white one who seemed friendly – at least she wasn't so tall.

"Meow!" greeted Cannelle and waited. Cats always say "meow" first, pretending they don't know how to speak to gain the upper hand.

"Maa, maa," replied the little white goat.

"I see you're still little, but the right word is meow, not maa!" corrected Cannelle.

"Maa," replied the goat, bending her head down to nuzzle Cannelle in a show of affection.

The cat stretched a paw out and gently stroked the animal's forehead. "Never mind maa or meow, let's be friends! What's your name?"

"Goat, Little White Goat," replied the animal. "And who are you?"

The friendship was sealed, and the conversation began. They lay down on the grass and told each other their life stories. The only missing was tea for two with scones; a little butter would also have been appreciated. Cannelle asked if there were some cat restaurants nearby.

"No," replied the goat, "there aren't any restaurants, not even a fry shack. Which is a shame because we love salt!"

As it was already getting late, the kitty left. However, she promised to return as soon as possible – with salt if she happened to find any.

She went back to the B&B, her "home" now, and decided to resume her search for Bins, the famous restaurant where they supposedly served food scraps.

Tough Times

It was easy to find Bins now: Cannelle could hear the cats arguing behind the B&B, not far from the kitchen. However, when she reached the place, there was no way she could get near the food! The area was overcrowded; two large tomcats reigned supreme and chased the small ones away.

Cannelle had to wait late into the night before the crowd began to disperse. Once they were gone, all she found were two dehydrated bread croutons. Well, better than nothing, she thought and carried them away to enjoy her modest dinner.

She decided the next day that Bins wasn't the right place for her, nor were the kitchen or the dining room. She had to find something else.

What about the tables on the garden terrace? The guests liked having a drink and a snack in the garden. Staying close, rubbing around ladies' legs and playing with kids were strategies that paid off. The piece of croissant or a small slice of ham or cheese that fell to the ground from time to time helped her survive.

Squatting around the parking lot was her second-best tactic, although she had to be very careful not to get run over. But the advantage was evident: as soon as guests arrived, they would notice her. Sometimes they would give her a little leftover sandwich or cake. But sadly, it happened rarely, and the kitten was getting thinner and thinner.

Tough times arrived with the end of the tourist season. Cannelle's target market shrank like a wet ball of wool. The guests stopping over at the B&B now were primarily businessmen, too busy with their mobile phones to notice the hungry little kitten.

Sometimes Cannelle would have nothing to eat for three or four days in a row. She had become so thin that her life was in danger.

And yet, Cannelle lost neither her good humour nor her optimism. She knew that the big day was near; her new Mum would soon come to pick her up, she was sure. And then she would take her to a house where there would be plenty to eat all the time, day and night.

Almost every afternoon, she visited the little white goat to share with her the expectations of this happy event to come.

"You know, soon she'll come and take me with her."

"Maa," replied the goat.

"Yes, my new Mum! You know that too, don't you?" Cats, like humans, hear what they want to hear.

"I am a princess, and my castle is waiting for me. My new Mum will take me there soon; she'll come in her car, and we'll drive off." Then she looked at the little goat and added, "Don't be sad, my lovely friend! You'll come with us. My Mum has a lot of salt in her kitchen."

And guess what? She was right! Except for the salt. And the fact that it wasn't Mum but rather my human brother, Harry, who arrived.

Finally, He Came!

It was an afternoon like any other. Cannelle was lying in the shade of a big tree, far too weak to visit her friend, the goat. She was waiting for dinner time when she would go to the big steps hoping someone would throw her a little something.

A black car arrived, drove slowly across the parking lot and stopped not far from her. At first, Cannelle ignored it; cars came and went almost all day, especially in the evening. The newcomers seldom paid attention to the cats –busy with their luggage, their main concern was registering and finding their room.

However, almost as soon as the engine stopped, she heard steps approaching and felt someone behind her. A young man leaned over and stroked her gently. "What are you doing here, little kitty? How thin you are!"

Cannelle was surprised: how come someone suddenly noticed her and was nice to her? She turned her head to have a look– oh, surprise! It was him, her new human brother! Of course, Cannelle had never met him before and didn't even suspect he existed. But looking at him now, she was sure - her Mum had sent this young man to pick her up and to take her to her forever home!

"Are you my human brother?" She asked and, without waiting for the reply, started rubbing her head against his legs. "Where have you been? I've been waiting here for ages! Why are you so late?"

Harry, not yet used to Cannelle's accent, believed the kitty was asking for food. "I know, you're hungry!" he replied. "Does no one feed you here?"

He returned to his car, opened a bag, took out a cake sachet and offered a large cake to the kitty.

"I don't have anything else here," he said, "but I'll ask for something in the kitchen for you."

"No, meow, meow," cried Cannelle. "Don't ask! Don't go there! They'll hit you with a ladle!"

Did he understand? The kitty was afraid for him – one could expect just anything from that stupid Chef! But she seized the cake and retreated into a bush to devour the feast. It was a very large cake, and this was the biggest piece of food she'd received in a month! As soon as the meal was over, she emerged from the bush to ask for more. But Harry had already gone inside the B&B.

Never mind, thought Cannelle, *he'll come back; his car is still here.* She knew she would leave with her human brother, and he'd take her to her forever home, to her Mum. No, not the one who had abandoned her a month ago! Her genuine, loving Mum from whom she'd never part again. In the meantime, she had to tell the world that she would be leaving soon. Happy times were ahead, and Cannelle jumped, danced and sang all afternoon in the gardens.

When the evening came, she returned to the parking lot to search for her new human brother. But oh, what a deception! He was nowhere to be seen. Even his car had left!

This just cannot be true, thought the distressed kitty. This was even more disappointing than the first abandonment!

What to do now? To return to the big steps and beg for a piece of food? Or to go and face the gang of hungry cats at Bins? Should she dare enter the dining room again and risk being kicked? Undecided but very hungry, she walked in the direction of Bins. Maybe there was a bread crust left, or even an old chicken bone. Perhaps she would have some luck tonight.

Just as she turned the corner of the mansion, she heard a voice calling, "Kitty, kitty! Where are you? Come, come to eat!"

Cannelle was startled – this was the voice of her human brother! Not only was he back, he even had food! She ran across the lawn to join him with little mews and jumps. "Come with me to my room," said her brother. And without any further formalities, he gently lifted Cannelle and carried her away, talking to her. "You know, the people here are mean and don't allow guests to feed cats. But I drove to the city and bought plenty of food for you. Let's go to my room and have a feast! Would you like to do that?"

Of course, Cannelle agreed! She could smell good cat food in his bag, and besides, it was so lovely to be held by someone who cared for her.

His room was in the outbuildings, with the door opening directly to the garden. How convenient for the little cat! Once inside, they unpacked the food (Cannelle helped – she was pretty good at unpacking). Dear, dear! There were packets of cat biscuits, ham, treats, vet food and even cat milk! He had thought of everything: he'd even brought saucers and bowls! In no time, the kitty's dinner was served.

Imagine Cannelle's joy! She started to eat immediately. Her happy brother watched her, smiling. It was so rewarding to see the starved kitty devouring her meal! She kept eating for hours, it seemed to him. She did stop from time to time, though, just for a head rub and a tiny meow to express her gratitude. When the dinner was over, she stretched out on the big soft bed next to her newly acquired brother for more cuddles and kisses.

"When will we go home to Mum?" she asked, but her brother, tired from the long trip, was already asleep.

Farewell to the B&B

After sharing breakfast with her brother the following morning, she went out to have a run in the gardens. She was so happy! "Don't go too far," recommended Harry. "We will be leaving in the early afternoon." He had no idea whether the cat would want to go with him or how to carry her as he hadn't brought a cat carrier. He was wrong of course. One should always have a cat carrier in the car, just in case.

The morning passed calmly. Cannelle was happier than she had ever been. She jumped around, raced against herself and went butterfly hunting. Suddenly, she remembered her friend, the little white goat. *She has to come with us. I'll go and fetch her*! Thought Cannelle and headed towards the meadow, a bit anxious.

Would the goat be there? Sometimes she wasn't, but today, she saw a white spot from the distance and ran to her friend.

"Hey," said Cannelle. "You know, he's arrived!"

"Maa," replied the goat.

"No, Mum isn't here, but my human brother came to take me to her! And he has a car! He will drive both of us away."

She rubbed her back around the goat's legs, and the goat returned the affection with her wet muzzle.

"Get ready; we're leaving soon! Come, we'll be so happy at Mum's house! This place here is full of ladles, brooms and kicks! And you know, Mum has plenty of salt – you told me you like salt, didn't you?"

"Maa," repeated the goat, rubbing her head against Cannelle.

"Won't you come?"

Why wasn't her friend showing any joy? The goat continued to graze the grass as if nothing had happened. "This is our big day! Come, hurry up, where's your stuff? I'll help you pack!"

Finally, the little white goat replied: "I can't leave without my mummy and daddy, my brothers and sisters and my aunties and uncles, my cousins, my grandparents, and my great-grandparents, and. . . ."

Cannelle was taken aback. "But how many of you are there?"

"I don't know. Many! Sometimes we cover the whole pasture as far as you can see."

"Oh dear, oh dear!" Cannelle was distraught. "Well, my bro's car isn't big enough to carry so many of you." Suddenly her joy at leaving was tinged with sadness. Tenderly, she looked at her friend. Should she leave her forever? The thought seemed unbearable But it only lasted a moment because Cannelle was a highly optimistic kitty.

"You know what? We'll come back for you. I saw huge cars on the highway, as big as a house! I think they're called trucks. My bro surely has one!"

Suddenly she realised she was running late. Maybe her brother had gone away without her? She quickly gave the goat a last kiss. "Take care of you, little friend! We will be back soon. You'll see!" And she ran away, a bit worried. Would the car have left without her? It could not happen. It must not happen!

As for Harry, he had spent the morning attending to business. After lunch, he started packing.

He was ready to leave by mid-afternoon, but the kitty was nowhere to be seen. It was time to hit the road to avoid the heavy traffic near Paris. He looked every-where for the cat, called, went around the gardens and asked some people to help look. But in vain. Cannelle had disappeared. He didn't want to leave this little kitten behind; he had noticed how cats were treated here, and then this little one was so skinny that she wouldn't survive very long.

"She'll probably be back when it's dark," suggested one person helping with the search.

"Maybe late at night," said another.

Unsure, Harry sat behind the wheel. Should he leave now and come back in a few days? But suddenly he saw her – Cannelle!

The kitty arrived out of nowhere at full speed, as if running for her life. Harry quickly opened the back door, and Cannelle jumped straight onto the back seat. She settled in comfortably.

"Meow!" she said. "Meow!" Which, of course, meant let's go, what you're waiting for!

Harry started the engine. Then he suddenly remembered that there was something else he needed to do, something important: it was time to warn Mum!

He called home. "I'm leaving now. I should be home for dinner."

"Great! Be careful, and don't speed too much!" replied Mum.

"But we are two," answered Harry and handed his mobile phone to Cannelle.

"Meow Mum, it's me! I'm coming, get the treats ready!" shouted Cannelle who had no doubt that she was welcome.

Mum laughed. "Ah, there are two of you! Then come on! We are waiting for you."

The journey lasted two long hours, and the kitty slept peacefully without moving once. Why worry? The hard times were over, she could relax. From now on, Mum will take care of her.

It was only when the car was approaching Mum's house that she stood up and started meowing: she knew it, her forever home was near.

A Striking Arrival

Back at home, we all learnt well in advance that Harry was on his way home, with a new kitty. Mum had told us to be ready to welcome her. We were so excited! Everyone wanted to give her a present.

"Another kid, I will have another kid!" sang our mummy cat Tahiti. Tahiti believes all the kittens for miles around are her kids. She searched in her treasure box and decided she would offer "her new baby" the green ribbon, her preferred one.

Daddy cat Uddy was digging in our toy box. "We will give her some of our cutest toys," he declared.

We thought this was a brilliant idea.

"Yes, I'll get her my red mousie!" said Vanille.

Vicky brought the stuffed rainbow toy from under the sofa, where she'd stashed it for special occasions. As for me, I ran into the garden and dug out the beautiful bird feather I had been saving for Mum's birthday. I was sure Mum would understand.

When we heard the car engine approaching and saw the big garden gate slowly opening, we were standing in our welcome formation at the door, ready to greet her. There were eight of us: seven giant Maine Coons and me, Freddy. The car stopped in the garden, and Harry stepped out.

"She's still so small; she will probably be scared when she sees our big cats. What should we do? What is the best way to introduce her?" he asked Mum.

She didn't have time to answer. The new kitty – we learned her name was Cannelle – jumped out of the car and came straight over to us.

All the Maine Coons greeted her with kind meows, "Welcome, little one!"

I didn't. I saw the disapproval in the kitten's eyes and whispered, "Woe, danger, beware!"

Unfortunately, nobody was listening to me. Cannelle walked calmly from one Maine Coon to the next and gave each one a big slap. A slap to Daddy Uddy's cheek! A slap to Mummy Tahiti's cheek! And so on. She slapped every single one of them. I didn't want to wait for my turn (I'm not a fan of slaps), so I ran and jumped over the rose bed and hid in the bamboo hedge. Phew, I was scared that she would come looking for me! But she didn't.

Once she had slapped the whole family, she went straight into the kitchen and finished all the leftovers we had kept for later.

It was only late in the evening that she finally bothered to speak to us. By then, I was back for dinner. You know, I never miss dinner at home!

"Big cats," she said, "what are you doing here? Get out of my house! This is my home, my castle, my Mum!"

I wanted to protest that I wasn't a "big cat"; I was just a kitten, like her. But in solidarity with the others, I didn't say anything. Of course, given the general mood, we decided by mutual agreement to postpone the presentation of the gifts.

That night and every night since, Cannelle has slept with Mum, holding Mum's arm firmly between her forepaws. This is because she's afraid Mum will go away and leave her in a parking lot like her first family did. But she needn't worry. Our Mum loves us all far too much.

I quickly forgave Cannelle for her outrageous behaviour when she first arrived, and we have become great friends. We're thinking of going back to that B&B; we need to bring that little goat home. She's waiting for us. I've checked in the kitchen – fortunately, we have plenty of salt for her. And she will be so helpful! No more of that horrible lawn-mower noise: the little white goat will graze on all grass in the garden. I can't wait to get her here!

CANNELLE

The Hedgehog Who Knew How to Ask for Help

One late afternoon as I was returning home from my patrol, I spotted something at our front door. Something small, round, and beige-brown in colour. I thought it was a large chestnut in its dried pod, but it started moving from right to left on the mat. Strange, I thought; I don't recall seeing chestnuts run. But who knows. . .? I figured I'd get closer and check, cautiously approaching it. If it could run, it could also bite or drive its quills into me – there are so many strange things in this world! My Mum is one. She believes my book is going to become a bestseller, poor thing! But let's move on.

A few steps from the front door, I realised it wasn't a chestnut – it was a tiny baby hedgehog!

"What are you doing here, *petit*? Where is your Mum?"

He seemed astonished by my question. "Mum? She's in the house! She'll be bringing my dinner soon."

"No," I said, "I mean your Mummy hedgehog. Where is she?"

"I love Mum! I'm your brother!" he replied and ran to the azalea flower bed to hide. I had the feeling he was emotional and was going to cry.

What was all this about, I wondered. Maybe I shouldn't have asked him this question. Perhaps the Maine Coons knew something about this? I thought I'd better go inside and speak with them. I jumped on the patio fence and from there onto the windowsill as I always do. The Maine Coons were already sitting around their plates and enjoying the dinner. It looked good and smelled delicious, so I joined them, forgetting about the baby hedgehog.

I remembered him only much later when we gathered around Mum for evening cuddles.

"The baby!" I exclaimed. "Did he get his dinner?"

Mum knew at once whom I was talking about. "Yes, Freddy, he gobbled a full plate of cat biscuits and ham!"

Daddy cat Uddy, who had seemed to be in a deep sleep, suddenly raised his head. "The baby? What baby? Mum, you haven't adopted someone new without telling us, have you?"

He was alarmed – and rightly so. Our Mum can adopt just about anybody and anything, not only birds and cats, but also ants, snails, butterflies, trees, and plants. When she goes to the garden centre, she probably asks the flowers around her, "Which one of you wants to come to my garden?" And I'm sure she genuinely expects a reply.

A little embarrassed, Mum told us the whole story. Here it is:

A few days ago, I enjoyed some fresh air on the patio. The evening was beautiful and calm, the last rays of sunlight illuminated the garden, and the birds were chirping everywhere. I hadn't had time to go out that day, so I just stood there, savouring this tiny moment of peace. The garden seemed empty. You'd all gone back into the house already, and our stray visitors hadn't yet arrived to ask for dinner.

Usually, hedgehogs come out of the bamboo hedge to quench their thirst at that time of the day. There is always fresh water available so that stray cats, birds, hedgehogs, and occasionally bees and butter-flies can drink. Our Freddy, who drinks the water from any puddle he finds (don't you, sonny?), showed me how precious water is to free-roaming animals.

It's then that I spotted them: a couple of hedgehogs running on the path. The first was a huge mummy hedgehog, possibly an older lady, which suddenly emerged from the flower bed and quickly ran towards the water bowl. She was followed by a tiny baby, her son, I supposed. I'd never seen them before, and I'm sure you would say the same. We know all the hedgehogs that come to our garden, don't we? But this pair was new to me. Mummy hedgehog ran so fast that it was difficult for the baby to follow her, yet he tried very hard.

She didn't care, didn't look back to see where the baby was and didn't wait for him. On the contrary, I felt she was doing everything to lose him. What strange behaviour! Usually, hedgehogs are always so attentive to their kids! Maybe she was very thirsty, I thought.

Once she reached the water bowl, she leaned over and started to drink. The baby finally caught up with her and tried to climb on her back. He clung to her back leg, but she shook herself vigorously, and the poor baby fell off.

He tried once, twice, three times, and she shook herself each time to get rid of him. Visibly very upset, she stopped drinking, turned to the baby, pushed him away with her paw, and ran towards the flower bed. The baby ran after her, and although she was running very fast, he managed to catch up with his mummy just before she disappeared into the foliage. Again, he clung to her leg, hanging onto her side. He wanted his mother to carry him so badly! It was probably what she usually did, and he likely couldn't understand why he wasn't allowed to be on her back now. Again, she shook herself to toss him off, but he tried again. This time, she paused and gave him a big kick with her back paw. The impact was so brutal that the little hedgehog ended up on his back, lying on the grass next to the path. By the time he managed to get on his feet, his mummy had disappeared inside the flower bed.

Poor baby! I ran to help him, but when I reached the spot, he too was gone. I assumed he had followed his mother. You can imagine how sorry I was for this tiny little being! What could I do? I searched the rhododendron bush all over but couldn't find either the baby or the mummy hedgehog. So, I went into the kitchen to fetch some cat biscuits and placed them on a plate next to the flower bed even though I doubted this little baby would eat by himself.

My darlings, I didn't tell you all this before because I knew it would make you sad. But I'm guessing you're now wondering how this baby became your brother.

The next evening, I wanted to check on the two hedgehogs. Would they come back? Had the mother been in a bad mood the day before? Had she changed her mind and become nice to her son? I hoped to see her reconciled with her baby and would have been so glad to see her carrying him on her back!

I stood still on the patio and waited without making the slightest noise for a long time. I didn't want to frighten them if they came back. After an hour or so, I wanted to go inside to make dinner for you, my kitties, but just then, my phone rang. I answered the call, which lasted some time, and forgot about watching for the hedgehogs.

Then suddenly, I felt something – or someone – climbing on my sneaker. Looking down, I saw him, the tiny little hedgehog, the baby! He was sitting quietly on one of my sneakers. He didn't seem frightened. He just raised his little muzzle towards me and tilted his tiny head to better look at me. Although I didn't hear him say anything, I'm sure he asked if I had something to eat.

I could hardly believe it. Had he sensed that I was worried about him? Had he guessed I was his best chance of survival?

Because he was tiny, he could squeeze through the narrow patio's fence. However, getting off the paved path, coming inside, and finding me must have required a lot of effort from such a tiny baby. Was it just a coincidence, or was he looking for me? When I'd placed the bowl of cat biscuits close to the flower bed, I had left a bit of my scent. This baby, who had probably eaten a biscuit or two, would likely have been looking for the same scent the next day when he got hungry.

He let me remove him gently from my sneaker, and I went to the kitchen to fetch some food.

"Don't move; wait for me right there!" I said as if he could understand me. I was back with finely chopped ham a few minutes later, served on a flat saucer. I thought the ham would be easier to chew than the biscuits.

He was waiting for me, running around the patio as if it were a fun game. Sniffing the corners, chair and table legs, he seemed as happy as a little kitten exploring his new surroundings. I put the plate next to a chair, and it didn't take him more than a few seconds to spot the food. First, he tasted a piece or two and, finding the ham to his liking, climbed right onto the plate. Then, sitting cosily in the middle, he devoured all the food around him. You will have to teach him a few things, now that he's your brother; for example, the plates aren't made to sit on!

Once he'd finished his dinner, I expected him to return to the flower bed, which I supposed was his home, but he didn't! He just stayed there, in a corner, too happy to have found a new home and a new Mum! The fox from the park sometimes comes to the patio at night, as you know. So I took the baby to the terrace, where it's more sheltered. Have you seen the crate next to the garage, Freddy? I'd lined it with straw for the rabbits I bought from the garden centre, and he's in there now, happy as a clam.

That's the whole story, my darlings. I hope you don't mind having a new brother!

Of course, we didn't mind. On the contrary, we were delighted! We all wanted to greet him and cuddle him at once. (Mum said that young baby hedgehogs have soft fur, like kitties, rather than spiky quills.) But Mum told us it was late and we should let him sleep. After all, we'd see him the next day.

So, the following morning, we organised a big party to celebrate Thad's arrival into the family. And that's how I became the big brother of a little hedgehog named Thad the Chestnut (as a reminder of my mistake).

Every evening, Thad comes to the front door to claim his dinner; if Mum isn't home or doesn't open the door immediately, he stands right up against the door and knocks gently on the glass with his muzzle.

"Where's my dinner, Mum? I'm hungry!" he calls, but only I can understand him.

We're brothers, but we're also the best of friends! We explore the hedges together and patrol all around the garden. If that rascal Big Head arrives, we face him off together. Um, I mean, we run away together to escape.

Oh, just another thing: the other day, I saved his life! It was before noon when I noticed he was missing. I looked everywhere in the garden – in the hedges, in his crate. . . He wasn't anywhere! So, I set out to explore the area. And that's when I found him, on the road to Paris. Well, what I saw first was a truck driving very slowly. Then I saw Thad walking right in front of the big engine, with the utmost calm.

"Thad, you little fool, what are you doing?" I cried.

"I'm going to look for my hedgehog Mummy. I heard she went to Paris to get some jam for breakfast."

Gee, I don't know who could have told him such a silly thing. I meowed very, very loudly, and the truck driver heard me. He stopped his giant machine to see what was going on. I quickly jumped next to Thad, trying to push him out of the way, but I couldn't. The truck driver, a lovely man, stepped out, picked both of us up at the same time in his enormous hand, and put us on the side of the road, on the grass.

Mind you, he did reprimand us a little bit, but we probably deserved it, didn't we?

Now that I know Thad would love to have his hedgehog Mummy back, the Maine Coons and I have imagined a plan to help him. But I'll tell you more about that next time!

Princess Pearl Goes to London

Pearl ran into our garden one stormy night.

Of course, I wasn't outside to welcome her; I was indoors, cowering under the bed. The yellow monster arrived suddenly and thundered in the sky, tearing it apart with its blinding light. It was looking for me again, so I had to hide.

"Where is that Freddy, that rascal?" it seemed to be yelling. "I'm going to swallow him up all in one gulp! Hey, you people down there, have you seen Freddy?"

And it thundered and thundered. Oh, my ... that was something to be afraid of, wasn't it? But please, if it asks you about me one day, say you don't even know me. Say something like, "Freddy? Who's that? A frog? A rabbit?"

As I said, I couldn't greet Pearl under these circumstances, but Mum did it for me. She had gone out to check that all the cats were safe. It was raining heavily. While talking to Lulu, who was reluctant to come inside, she heard a car approaching slowly. It stopped right in front of the garden gate. She wondered who could be coming to call at this late hour. When she heard the car door open and close, she expected someone would ring the bell. But the car started up again and quickly moved off.

A few seconds later, Mum heard desperate meows, and suddenly, there she was: a big white kitty snuggling up against Mum's legs with her wet fur. Those people in the car had stopped only to dump the poor cat in front of our garden.

"Meow," cried the cat loudly. "Here I am! Where is my dinner?" They didn't even feed her before they ditched her, and she was starving.

Mum offered her all the leftovers from the cats' dinner outside, but, as this didn't seem enough, she went to the kitchen to get some more, adding treats. She deserved it, the poor girl. She also brought back a towel to rub and dry her wet fur.

"Poor darling, do you want to stay here?" she asked – out of politeness. She already knew the answer.

That's how the following day, I found a beautiful white cat in the hallway, sleeping in my basket near the heater. I asked her who she was and what she was doing in my house. Nothing unpleasant, just to know. But she replied harshly.

"Your house? You have to understand, you little dummy, that this house is mine from now on. You'll remain here only if I want you to."

I was about to raise my paw to teach her who was boss when Mum came in with the carrier.

"Oh, Freddy, please be kind to the poor kitty! I'm taking her to the vet, and if we don't find her owner soon, she may become your sister. You have to be nice to her."

Pearl, of course, made an innocent face and even produced a plaintiff meow as if to say, "Mum, he was going to hit me!" A likely story! What a little minx that girl is – as if she couldn't defend herself: she is almost twice as big as me!

The vet said she wasn't chipped, was still pretty young, and was in good health. Mum started to look around for the owner, but she couldn't find anybody who might know her. No one had ever seen this beautiful white cat with little calico spots around the ears and on the tail. She could hardly have gone unnoticed, as you will see a little further on: she is a cat with bags of personality. After two weeks of searching in vain, Mum took her back to the vet to be chipped. Mum named her Pearl because of her shiny white fur.

But do you think this improved her mood?

Ha! Now that she knew she had a forever home, it became even worse. She decided to chase all cats out of the garden, except Big Head – naturally, one needs to assess the risks. I couldn't complain too much; sometimes, she even helped me with my patrols in the neighbourhood. But Fifi, Caramel, and all the other cats in the garden had to be constantly wary of her. My half-brother Joey didn't dare to come to dinner until very late in the evening, once Pearl had gone inside to sleep. I felt sad for him, as I love him very much. Strangely enough, Pearl never got involved with the Maine Coons. On the contrary, she liked to lie next to Vanille, Vicky, or Daddy Uddy and cuddle up with Mummy Tahiti.

"Pearl," I asked her, "why do you hate all the cats except the Maine Coons?"

"Maine Coons? Do you mean those big animals, Mummy Tahiti and Daddy Uddy? Don't be so silly, Freddy! They're not cats!"

As I didn't want to disappoint her, I didn't pursue the matter. What can you expect from a cat who thinks she's a dog? Every morning she waits impatiently for Mum to set out for her trip to the shops. Then she runs to the garden gate, ready to escort her.

"Meow, meow," she calls loudly from there. "Hurry up, Mum! I want my croissant and slices of ham! We're late! There may not be any left!"

Then they both set off, striding along the street, Pearl two steps behind Mum. Passers-by stop to admire them.

Their first stop is the supermarket. Mum goes in to do her shopping while Pearl waits outside in the doggy place. If there is a bowl of water for dogs, she laps up some of it to show she knows how to behave like a dog.

The next stop is the bakery. Again, as dogs aren't allowed inside, Pearl waits on the pavement. Sometimes, the baker offers her half a croissant, which she gladly accepts, gobbling it up greedily in front of the shop while Mum is served a coffee. She also gets a piece of Cheddar or Camembert at the cheese shop, her favourites. In no time, our Pearl has become a local celebrity.

Pearl lets Mum know it's time for the race home when all the shopping is done. After three prompts, "Meow, meow, meow!" to give the start, she turns and gallops off through the gardens.

Of course, she is the first back home. As Mum approaches the house, she sees Pearl already waiting for her at the garden gate, proud and happy to have won again. Yet it seems to me with a bit of a disdainful expression.

You might think from this that Pearl is happy with us. But actually, she isn't really. Her greatest aim in life is to become a "unique cat" – something I could not even imagine. Goodness, this must be so boring!

"You see, Freddy", she said to me the other day, "I will soon become a princess, the sole cat in my kingdom. And then I'll make sure the guy who dumped me outside your gate that stormy night knows all about it. I'll put it on all the social networks – he'll be so furious! And all newspaper banners will shout, "From Dumped Cat to Princess". Ha! A nasty man! That will serve him right!

"But how does one become royalty?" I asked, a little jealous, despite myself. If it's easy, maybe I could become a prince too. Well, without ever leaving my magic garden, of course.

"First, you need to move out of a republic to a kingdom. There is one, just across the Channel, I've heard. And it's so beautiful! Imagine, Freddy, they have red double-decker buses, red phone booths, and – incredible but true – some people wear bears on their heads. They are called Guards."

I was astonished, as you can imagine. "Bears on their heads?"

"Yes, Freddy, black bears! I want one too – it keeps you warm, and you can cuddle it and engage in a little chat.""

"And what's it called, this kingdom?"

"United Catsdom. They're waiting for me, you know. I'll have my castle in the city centre, with a garden bigger than yours, Freddy. An old lady, the senior princess, is waiting for me, and I will have ten servants and golden baskets lined with bear fur arranged all around my palace."

I let her talk but didn't believe a word, as you can imagine. Who would think there is a country with double-decker buses and red phone booths? And this fishy story about bears being made into hats! She was just pulling my leg, wasn't she?

But, strangely enough, Mum got a letter from a lady in central London who wanted to adopt Pearl. She lives in a big house with a beautiful garden, she wrote. I'm not sure if this is the place Pearl dreams about or if she really wants to go there. Anyway, how will she get her freshly baked croissant in the morning if she does go? She'll surely miss that. And she'll miss me too, won't she? I'm sure she loves me, even if she teases me quite a lot. I have to confess I love her too. Well, just a little bit.

PEARL

Chapter Four

IN WHICH A TINY KITTEN FEEDS ON GRAVEL TO
SURVIVE, AN OLD LADY RISKS HER LIFE TO HELP
CATS, AND A MOTHER CAT PERFORMS A
REMARKABLE FEAT. AND IN WHICH A LITTLE
GIRL ADOPTS A WILD FOREST CAT (OR MAYBE
IT'S THE OTHER WAY AROUND).

A Pile of Sand That
Could Meow

While I was quietly resting on the couch on a rainy afternoon, my cousin Chili suddenly started talking. And the more he spoke, the more I felt like I was following him on his incredible journey.

So, Freddy, you asked me to tell you the story of my life. You wanted to know how I went from a pile of yellow sand to a beautiful cat – at least, according to what everyone says. I don't remember everything precisely, but I have a pretty good idea of the essential bits.

One early morning, just after I'd had my breakfast, my Mummy cat said, "Littledarlin" (You see, Freddy, this was my name back then)"'Littledarlin, I'm off to get some food. You go to sleep now, and when you wake up, I'll be right here next to you."

"And we will play together, Mummy, and you will let me get more mil?" I was so little that I couldn't say 'milk' yet.

"Of course, my baby, I'll have much more milk after finding some food!"

Mummy smiled and kissed me on the head. She helped me curl close to the wheel on my little bed – you see, our house had four wheels and an iron roof. It was convenient as the sun couldn't come in and bite my skin, and the raindrops fell all around but never inside. I was so tiny that I didn't yet have a lot of fur to protect me, so I preferred to stay inside. Besides, I loved our home. Just too bad we didn't have one of those cosy baskets I see everywhere in your house. Mummy had to sleep on a stone floor, but she had arranged a little bed made of dry leaves for me.

As my belly was full of Mummy's good milk and I felt comfy, I immediately fell asleep.

I don't know how long my nap lasted, but I had the feeling it was very, very long. Of course, I expected to see Mummy next to me when I opened my eyes. But she wasn't there. I started calling for her by meowing as loudly as I could. There was no reply, so I got up, ran all over our home, from right to left, then back and forth, inspected the other three wheels, and looked outside by crawling along the boundaries.

Mummy was nowhere to be found; she didn't reply to my calls no matter how desperate they were. I was stunned; this was unusual. Whenever I'd wake up, she would be bending over me, her loving face looking at me.

What to do? Should I go back to my little bed and get more sleep until she returns? I decided it wouldn't work for me because I was so anxious. I had to go and look for my Mummy. Maybe she was lost. I had to bring her back home. Perhaps the food she had found was too heavy for her to carry, so I would have to help her. Or maybe she was feeling tired as she often did, so I had to take care of her. She needed me. You see, Freddy, you have plenty of sisters and brothers and cousins and friends and a Mum and a human brother, but we only had one another, Mummy and I. Besides, I was starting to feel hungry again.

Feeling brave, I stepped out into the vast new world. I'd never been there before! Boy, how bright it was! I had to close my eyes. But after a short while, I started getting used to it. *"En avant, petit,"* I said to myself and started to run straight ahead. My Mummy fancied speaking a little French from time to time. She had probably guessed that one day, France would become my new country. You see, Freddy, I was born in a very distant country where it never gets cold. Your human brother's family were there for an extended holiday with your cousin Dex.

I ran and ran and ran – towards the brightest spot, the sun. They say that lost kitties and kids always follow the sun. After a while, my paws started aching. Sharp gravel bit my toes, hurting me, and I had to stop and lick them to help them heal. But I had to go on. I had to find my Mummy. I kept running. *Mum must have gone a long way!* I thought when I noticed dusk falling.

Maybe she's back home by now and waiting for me, I thought. Suddenly I imagined her looking for me and calling me. "Mummy, Mummy", I answered and started to run in the opposite direction, back to our house.

To cut a long story short, Freddy, I couldn't find my way back to my home on wheels. First, a big dog wanted to make his dinner out of me – at least he seemed to. I only narrowly escaped. Then a large tomcat warned me to "Get the hell out of here before I tear you apart!" Because I didn't want him to do this, I quickly ran away. Then, some human kids tried to catch me by calling me "Kitty, kitty!" But I wasn't "kitty"; I was Littledarlin. So I had to run again.

The night had fallen, and neither my Mummy nor my house was anywhere to be found. I was also so, so hungry! Exhausted, unable to stand up anymore, I lay down. The sand was soft and warm, almost as smooth as Mummy's fur. I ate some of it. It was nowhere near as good as Mummy's milk, but it filled my belly, so I buried myself inside it to sleep.

I woke up several times during the night and called," Mummy, my mil, I want my mil! Mummy, please, I'm so hungry!" I hoped to see her sweet face just above me and couldn't believe she wasn't there. Freddy, I really couldn't understand it, couldn't accept it. All I saw was a dark sky with plenty of bright stars.

Hot rays of the sun woke me up early the following day.

My belly ached. I didn't know whether it was because of my hunger or the sand I'd eaten the night before. So I had a little more for breakfast while putting together my plans for the day. Where should I go, and which direction should I take? Suddenly, I had an idea: our house had wheels, remember? If I could find wheels, I would find my house and my Mummy in one go!

I had a lot of opportunities to find wheels that day. After running towards the rising sun, I quickly arrived at a hectic and noisy place – and found more wheels than I could ever imagine! I learned later that they were called 'cars,' and plenty of them were standing along a wide street. Crawling from under one to another, I inspected them all. Again and again, I called for my Mummy, asking for milk. I couldn't find her under them, not even after my second and third rounds.

I had to find more wheels. And I saw a lot more, but they were speeding down the road. I kept shouting, "Stop, stop! This is my house! Stop, I want my Mummy! Please give me my Mummy back! Meow!"

But do you think anyone stopped? Heartless things! They kept speeding past! I was so angry that I started to growl and hiss and spit at them as much as I could – from afar, of course. They seemed very dangerous.

* * *

Something suddenly made sense as Chili said that. I asked: "Ah, Chili, is that why even now, you want to attack every car you see?"

"You guessed it, Freddy! I'm still so mad at them for not giving me my Mummy back!"

I understood and let him continue his story:

I don't know how long I stayed on the side of that road. At night, I slept hidden in the sand; I inspected the parked cars and threatened those that wouldn't stop during the day. I ate small stones and a lot of soft sand to fill my belly. Sometimes I found a few blades of dried grass and feasted on them – they were so yummy! I didn't want to move from there. I was sure that, sooner or later, my Mummy would come because there were so many wheels!

Later, the vet told your human brother that I must have been lost for five or six days.

I felt so sad for Chili. I had to ask, "But she never came, your Mummy, did she? My poor friend. How unhappy you must have been! How much you must have suffered! If only I had known; I would have come and carried you to my home at once!"

Oh, Freddy, you can't even begin to imagine how frightening it was! Then one exceptionally bright and hot day, I decided I couldn't take it anymore. I was too tired to stay awake; my stomach hurt too much, and despite all the little stones I had swallowed that morning, I was still hungry.

So, I decided to write it off, cover myself up in the sand, sleep and never get up again. At least in my dreams, my Mummy would come. She did come often, only she was never there when I woke up. So I buried myself in the sand as deep as possible and fell asleep. I wanted to sleep until the end of the day, until the end of all days.

But I did wake up, and I found myself sitting in your cousin Dex's home, Freddy! I was wrapped inside a soft towel; I felt all fresh and wet. Someone had washed me! It felt as if I had just been born again. And I saw Dex and your Auntie Tamara, and Harry, your human brother, and I thought I had arrived in heaven. I asked for milk, got some, and was as happy as a clam.

But things went wrong quickly. They put me into a car and took me to someone called "vet". Oh, Freddy, how horrible! I had not one but three "stomach pumps", as they call it. It was because of all the stones, sand, and dust I had in my belly. It's very unpleasant. Trust me, Freddy, when I tell you this: don't ever eat sand!

Back at Dex's home, I wasn't feeling well. The vet had told my new family that I had little chance of staying alive. Your Auntie Tamara, now my new Mum, would often hold me against her chest, and I could feel how sad she was.

Then one morning, I said to myself, enough is enough. I have had enough sadness and misery! Now has come the time to live a happy life. To cheer up my new Mum, I climbed up next to her face and kissed her cheeks. And to show everyone how brave I was, I climbed on top of Dex's tree, Freddy! And he wasn't mad at me, on the contrary! He hugged me, touched my nose, licked my fur, and we became brothers.

CHILI AND DEX

* * *

"Wonderful, Chili! But how is it that Auntie discovered you when you were buried in the sand on that street?" I asked as this was unclear to me.

"It's because of my dream, Freddy!"

"Your dream? What do you mean?"

"You see, when I fell asleep there, I dreamt my Mummy came. I could see her. She was bending over me, whispering to me. She said, 'My poor little boy, my Littledarlin!' And I cried from happiness. I screamed, 'Mummy, meow, Mummy dear!' I guess your Auntie heard my screams, and she came to see how a pile of sand could meow.

So, that is the story of my life – you know the rest of it. As soon as I got better, I got all my vaccinations and my little passport, and we all flew to France, to my new forever home, to meet you.

"Yes, to play with my family and me and cuddle and be happy forever and ever, Chili!"

"Yes, Freddy. And that I am."

Angelina Dayan

CHILI

The Forgotten Cat

It all happened some time ago. Mum was still living in her tiny flat and had no cats. Incredible, isn't it? I can't imagine my Mum without a cat. Maybe it was because Dad said he didn't like cats. Well, that's what he thought back then because he'd never had any.

Sometimes, when the weather was nice on Sunday afternoons, they would go to their near-neighbour Raymond's little house. Mum would have taken her famous apple pie, freshly baked, with her; Raymond would set out three plates on the garden table and get ready tea for Mum. He preferred to open a good bottle of wine from his "own" vineyard for himself and Dad. (It was actually from his aunt's vineyard – she had an estate close to Bordeaux.) Of course,

Princess, a large tabby cat, would join them. She loved both apple pie and Mum's knees.

So, the four of them would sit there chatting all afternoon. Mum would cuddle Princess, who purred like an engine. Dad, who had always dreamed of being an adventurer (assuming this could be achieved without ever leaving his chair), would sip wine and drink in Raymond's words.

You see, Raymond, like me, was an adventurer. I dare to go as far as the park across the street! Of course, it's bold, please don't laugh at me! I have to avoid branches that scratch, tame snails, and chase away bees that want to kiss me. And let's not even mention the squirrels who are always demanding nuts.

Raymond had gone a bit further than the park; he went to a country where Siamese cats live, said Mum. He'd wanted to establish a vineyard and import wine to France. Still, the only thing he brought back was Princess.

Ah, Princess! According to Raymond, she was the daughter of a tiger, a relative of the King of Siam, an actual princess with a family line so famous that even the Queen of England was envious! Shortly, a cat so exceptional that all she lacked was the ability to speak – and even that was superfluous because

Raymond and Princess could understand each other just by exchanging a look.

Raymond told them he'd found Princess on the way to the jungle that stretched behind his house. She was just a tiny kitten then, crying for her mum, crawling here and there in the high grass. Some wild animal could have made a meal of her at any moment, a wild boar or a panther. Or a herd of elephants could have trampled her. She needed to be taken away. Raymond picked her up and brought her to his home. They lived happily on Raymond's property for two months, but it was time to flee one day. Unrest had broken out in the country, and the war was threatening. Raymond put Princess in his hand luggage, made holes for her to breathe, and issued the following travel advisory:

"Sweetheart, we're going to France. Don't say hello to the customs officers; they don't deserve it! "

Princess didn't have a passport yet, nor had she been issued an official identity document.

Princess, of course, understood the gravity of the moment. When arriving at the customs clearance at the airport, she remained silent. The zealous agents searched Raymond's suitcases from top to bottom – was he carrying some expensive antique, a precious carpet? But Raymond didn't desire ebony figurines and other trinkets; in his hand luggage was the only treasure he truly cared about: his Princess. Fortunately, nobody thought of searching for her. Once on the plane, he moved to a seat at the back as there was plenty of room and freed Princess. They spent the flight sharing meal trays and sleeping. Although he feared their arrival in Paris, they had incredible luck: the customs officers had just caught a big fish and ignored Raymond and Princess.

So, that's how Princess arrived in France: incognito. Of course, she was promptly taken to the vet, checked, and chipped.

Raymond introduced Princess to her new home – his tiny house close to Mum's flat. Then he went to the best pet shop and acquired such a large volume of baskets and toys and cat food that a shopkeeper had asked, "Oh, sir, you do have many cats, don't you?"

He forgot his dreams of a vineyard on the other side of the world and resumed his work - he was an engineer and worked in the same company as Dad, which is how they met.

Princess seemed happy to be alone. During the day, she explored her new garden, talked to the birds, and befriended a few cats and some friendly dogs. She liked to socialise. When Raymond got home from work at the end of the day, he would often find Princess on the doorstep, surrounded by a gang of meowing cats and wagging dogs: her guests for dinner.

On Fridays, Raymond would visit the fish shop to see if they had any leftovers for cats. On Saturdays, he would rush to the market to get the best roast chicken, moist and crispy, because that's how Princess liked it. If anyone asked him how he was doing, he would reply: "Thank you, Princess is doing well!"

Evenings, he would often pop into Mum and Dad's to share a glass of wine and occasionally dinner. Of course, he would talk about Princess. She filled his life, heart, and mind, and he would smile and laugh as he told them about her exploits.

But one day, something terrible happened.

It was a summer day towards the end of the holidays. Raymond and Princess had just spent a whole month on his aunt's estate and were on their way back to Paris. Not far from Bordeaux, Raymond decided to take a break. It was true that they had only travelled a short distance and that most of the road was ahead of them, but he had been working all day in the vineyard to help his aunt and was tired. He saw a pleasant resting place with a large oak tree and a wooden bench. What could be better, he thought and stopped. They both got out of the car and sat on the bench to share a takeaway, some delight from his aunt. Princess was like my Uncle Panda; she travelled freely without a carrier or leash. She followed her dad everywhere without any risk of getting lost. At least that's what Raymond thought.

After the meal, Princess went to chase butterflies in the high grass around them and stretch her paws, while Raymond allowed himself the luxury of dozing off "for a few minutes". Anyway, he thought, he wouldn't stop again until Paris.

When he finally woke up, it was almost dark. He called out to Princess, but she did not answer. He looked inside the car and noticed her shape curled up on the back seat, so he wished her a satisfying nap. "Off we go, sweetie, non-stop to your home!" he said and happily drove away.

It was almost midnight when he finally stopped in front of his house. He unloaded the luggage and was a little surprised when he didn't see his cat jump out and run into the house as she used to.

Was she too tired, sick maybe? He looked in the back seat.

Oh, what a shock! The shape he had taken to be Princess was only his jumper, which he'd thrown on the back seat. It was the same colour as Princess's fur. He searched further – under the seats and every-where in the garden. He called and called. But Princess was nowhere to be seen.

He wanted to set off immediately, to go back to that rest area, but he realised he was too tired. He decided to get a few hours of sleep first but woke up before dawn and drove as fast as he could, often exceeding the speed limit, all the way down to that rest area close to Bordeaux.

However, he had to drive back and forth before finding the exact spot: the big oak with the wooden bench. *She cannot be anywhere but here*, he thought. *She's probably hiding up on some high branch, waiting for me to come and rescue her.*

But he couldn't find her. Maybe she was at the very top of the tree, frightened, too afraid to come down? The branches were so numerous and the foliage so thick that a cat could easily be hidden.

If only I had been there; I would gladly have helped him! One, two, three, in no time, I would have been up at the top of that tree! I climbed up a very high poplar in the neighbour's garden one day. It was so high that it almost reached the sky! I was tiny then, and Mum had been afraid I wouldn't be able to get down. But I wasn't scared, no! I indeed meowed; however, it was only because I feared my garden would disappear. From way up, it had seemed so small! Mum had called the firefighters for help. But even before she could explain what was going on, I was already back on solid ground.

Anyway, I wouldn't have been of any help to Raymond that day as Princess wasn't up the tree; she wasn't anywhere around. No matter how long he searched in the tall grass, calling for her, he could not find her. He waited most part of the day, then drove to the nearby village to get a coffee and a few provisions as he wanted to spend the night at the rest area. Maybe she would come at dark, he thought. He also bought some cat food, thinking she would be pretty hungry by then. That night, he slept in his car with a window open. The slightest noise woke him up. *It's Princess*, he thought. He would call and wait, then, feeling despondent, fall asleep again. The following day, he decided to drive to his aunt's estate. What if Princess had gone back to her holiday place? After all, it wasn't very far away, and she had been so happy there, spoiled by his aunt.

His aunt was very sorry to hear what had happened. She had become used to the big tabby kitty who had followed her all summer. But no, she hadn't seen her. At least Raymond managed to get some rest, and his aunt's words sounded like a balm for the soul.

"Don't worry too much, my dear. Princess will be back soon. If you don't find her, she will find you! She loves you so much!" his aunt had said.

Raymond returned to the rest area; he spent another night in his car. The following morning, he went again to the nearby village to post notices about his lost tabby cat at all shops and then drove to Paris alone.

He had to go back to work but waited impatiently for the weekend to come when he would be free to drive back to that famous tree. He spent four weekends in a row under that oak, eating sandwiches, drinking coffee, and sleeping in his car. Occasionally, he would visit his aunt to get a bit of comfort.

Then the fifth weekend came. Would he go down to Bordeaux again, wait in vain with mad hope, and be disappointed anew? His courage failed him. He thought she wouldn't come back; "I would never see her again," he said to himself in a strangled voice.

As it was a Saturday, he went to the market and bought a roast chicken, crispy and moist, precisely as Princess liked it. Not that he felt like eating chicken; it was more in her memory.

As soon as he opened the garden gate at home, he saw her. The little shape of a cat on the doorstep, curled, obviously sleeping. Although she looked nothing like the beautiful tabby cat she had been before, he knew it was her, even from a distance. He called to her, and she raised her head and walked towards him, slowly, limping a little.

"Ah, you came back because you knew we'd have chicken for lunch!" said Raymond and took her in his arms.

Suddenly, the sun lit up his garden, and the birds started singing the most beautiful song ever. Suddenly, the whole world smiled at him. He kept kissing the cat, holding her so tightly that she let out a meow of protest. He began to dance with her, clenching her close to his face and humming. All of a sudden, life was so beautiful again.

After taking care of her, he called his aunt. He called Mum and Dad. He called his friends, some of whom didn't even know about the story. But it didn't matter; everyone had to know that Princess was back.

"The only cat in the world who would travel 300 miles to find her dad," said Raymond. Mum told me that was a bit of an exaggeration – for a start, it was only a little over 200 miles, and Mum had heard of other cats doing the same. But she didn't say anything to Raymond so as not to spoil his joy.

That day, after a good meal, Raymond took Princess to the vet for a check-up. She was doing well and needed nothing apart from food and a good bath. Only her claws had been worn down, and the pads on her feet were slightly injured. But the vet provided a healing pomade, and all was soon well again.

Shortly after this episode, Raymond arrived to share some big news: Princess was expecting kittens! We don't know if it was because of what had happened, but suddenly Dad changed his mind and agreed that one of Princess's kittens would come to live with them. It was Pomponette, an almost white kitty with a few black spots, the second cat Mum had in her life.

Dad fell head over heels for the tiny kitten from the first week onwards – the so-called man "who didn't like cats"! Whenever he didn't see her, he called: "Kitty sweetie, come to your Daddy!"

I've been thinking about this story, and you know what? I would have done the same as Princess – but even better: I would go to the ends of the earth to look for Mum. And wherever she was, I would find her.

Birthday Present

This story happened to my great-granddad, Jon.

It was a beautiful spring day, and Jon was walking up the mountain road to his daughter's home. She lived in a remote village a couple of miles away. Jon wasn't alone – four little kittens were with him. They were locked in a carrier basket, huddled together for courage, desperately meowing. They were still at home with their mummy cat only an hour ago! But then Jon came along with a big basket, grabbed them one by one and stuffed them inside something that looked like a cage. They called "Mummy, where are you? Come and get us!" But there was no reply. She always came; why didn't she answer their calls this time?

The last time they had heard their mother's voice was when she was running after the basket and begging Jon to let them free. Jon ordered her to return home, and the little ones had become even more frightened. Now all they could hear were Jon's heavy footsteps and his voice repeating over and over: "Keep calm, babies! We will be there soon!"

There? But where? What would happen to them? So many terrible things could happen to a kitten trapped in a carrier! A vet could suddenly come up and stick a needle in its back, or worse, it could be left in the middle of nowhere, at the mercy of some evil-minded tomcat. There was a tomcat hanging around in their garden sometimes.

As for Jon, he was getting tired. That road kept going up and up, and it had rained the day before, so it was all muddy. What an idea to live so high up in the mountains! If it hadn't been for Marianne, I would never have come! He thought.

Who was this Marianne for whom Jon was ready to go to great lengths? She was his granddaughter and that day was her birthday. The kittens were the present, a wonderful surprise for a little girl who loved cats.

Well, if everything were to go as planned.

After an hour's strenuous walk, Jon arrived at his daughter's house. Fortunately, Marianne was still at school. For a successful surprise, she was not to see the kittens until the afternoon, at her party.

Jon helped his daughter settle the little ones in the bathroom with fresh water, cat biscuits and toys. He noticed that the window was open, but it was located very high on the wall, near the ceiling, so there was no risk of the little ones escaping.

Jon gladly accepted a glass of white wine, chatted a little with his daughter, then said goodbye and headed back home.

He whistled and sang all the way down the mountain; it was a much more pleasant journey now. He rejoiced in how happy Marianne would be when she discovered her present.

He was still whistling as he entered his dining room. But there, he stopped short.

What an extraordinary scene!

In front of the fireplace, the four kittens were gathered around their mother, grooming themselves. How was this possible? How had they escaped from the bathroom? It seemed genuinely incredible.

First, he found it annoying - after all the effort he had to make to get up there! Moreover, they had over-taken him, arriving before him!

Then he laughed aloud: "So that's it, kids, you don't want to leave the house? You'll stay here with your Mum, as she loves you so much. I'm certainly not going to climb up there again!"

When his daughter called by later to claim the kittens, he advised her to go to the shelter. They certainly had plenty of cats to adopt there.

Of course, he promised to provide some other present for Marianne.

But what exactly had happened? How had the little ones managed to escape? No one knew precisely; however, there was a clue: on the bathroom wall under the window were the paw prints of an adult cat. The kittens' mother must have followed Jon up to his daughter's house. She had probably entered the bathroom through the open window and taken her kittens out, one by one.

Mum told me that this story had been a family joke for generations. When they wanted to get great-granddad a little bit roused, they asked him whether he would like to carry some kittens up the mountain.

I was, of course, not there, but I would have liked to meet these kittens and their loving mother.

The Old Lady

She comes out of her little house, holding a large jar. She is not very young; her back is stooped from years of toil in the fields. All the life she had lived here, in this house built by her great grandfather. It wasn't a palace, but it used to stand firm before the bombs rained down all around. There are no front door or window panes left, but that's not too bad. The old wood-burning stove is still working, and that's where she cooks dinner for the cats. And occasionally for herself.

As the bombing is approaching, rescue workers come to implore her:

"Babushka, come with us; it's time to leave. We need to get you to safety."

"I can't", she says, "Look, they are waiting for me." And with a waving hand, she points to the little group of cats. "They are lost, forgotten, left behind. They have no one else but me. Now they are my kids, you know."

Then she bends down and starts sharing the food of the jar into the small saucers: a spoonful for the old tabby Kathy, another one for the big ginger Roger, two spoonsful for the white Isabella who was ill, and so on. It's a little bit for everyone, and it doesn't matter if they are more than 20 and if there is almost nothing left for herself.

"Babushka, let's pack; we'll help you." Insists the security officer. "Russians are coming; you need to leave!"

The old lady looks at the little band of cats devouring their dinner. It's just porridge with a bit of milk and cream - that's all she has left. But it doesn't matter, it's cooked with love, and the cats enjoy it.

"I'll stay with them to the end; they need me." She says and smiles with tears in her eyes.

I watch her on the TV screen as she returns to her shaky house, and I think to myself:

She's not just some old lady with a little hump. She's a grande dame with a golden heart.

I need to ask Mum to find out exactly where her house is. And then I will go and visit her and bring her all my treats and a load of toys. And when dusk begins to creep in, I will sit on her old bench in the garden. There, amid all the cats, I will tell her the most beautiful story. A story that will make her laugh, a story so funny that even the sound of the bombs will become unnoticeable.

A story I have yet to write.

A Treasure in the Forest

Murray

Many years ago, when Mum was young, she lived with Granny and Aunt Ella in a small house on the edge of a large forest, far away from any village. It was in a very remote area, a sort of wilderness.

I asked Mum if they had a cat. It was undoubtedly a perfect place to explore for a kitty. I would have been so happy there – I would hardly ever have come home! But no, they didn't. At least not at the beginning of this story.

However, they did have a dog, Murray, who was so old that he had turned partly grey instead of being all black. Oh dear, he must have been at least a hundred years old! Or even two hundred.

One day, something terrible happened to poor Murray. A hunter took aim at him and fired a shot (I wonder if it was really accidental, as he later claimed?) The bullet touched the dog's skull. Murray, mad with pain, ran to hide in the forest with heart-wrenching screams, according to the other hunters who later described the event.

Unfortunately, there was no one at home when this happened. Mum was at school, and granny and aunt were at work. They discovered the traces of blood in the evening and went looking for Murray. He didn't answer their calls and was nowhere near the house.

It took three days to find him. He had hidden in a fox burrow, deep in the forest. Wounded, exhausted and starved, he was shaking and moaning, his voice hardly audible. They took him home, where granny first settled him in the car and then drove directly to the hospital in the nearby town where she worked-she was the head nurse. As she didn't know any animal care clinic in the area, she thought the best thing would be to take the dog to her colleagues in the hospital.

They didn't skip a beat and immediately took care of him. The surgeon cleaned the wound - fortunately, the bullet only grazed his skull – and they moved the dog to a quiet room for a few hours. Then granny returned home and took a week off to nurse him.

There was no question of leaving him alone outside again. Murray would go into the living room and lay in his comfortable basket, surrounded by toys and bowls filled to the brim with his favourite treats, whenever the family was away. Despite this incident and his already very old age, he lived for many more years. From an old dog who mainly had lived outside and to whom no one except Mum had ever demonstrated any real affection, Murray suddenly became a beloved doggy, a real pampered pooch – even though he did not look like one.

But life became even more exciting because he got some company shortly after that unfortunate event.

Kelly

That house on a clearing at the edge of the vast forest was an enchanting place for a little girl. Mum was then ten or eleven years old and marvelled at everything she saw around her, whether a colony of ants or a mother boar leading her kids in single file.

The deer with their mighty antlers would bell throughout the forest in autumn, ready to fight. Mum loved watching them. She would lurk breathlessly in the tall grass and follow their battles. Who would win? The old stag, so mighty that he looked scary, or the young one she liked to bet on? Of course, there was a risk of being trampled. Granny had forbidden her to get close. But it was so exciting! Mum said she would live every moment of the battle, trembling in fear for one or other of the stags.

It was even better than watching the wolves in winter. They sometimes besieged Mum's house. A pack of wolves would suddenly come running out of the forest and sit in a semicircle in the deep snow, not far from the house. Five or six, sometimes more, would remain there for hours. They would howl and show their menacing fangs. Venturing out was only possible after firing a shotgun in the air.

Summer was the bear season. A large brown one used to come on hot evenings to drink from the lake. He would pretend not to notice Mum, who liked to linger on the lake's shores. Why worry about a tiny girl when you are an impressive bear? The bear probably thought that just one puff would topple her.

I don't know if Mum was very brave or unaware of the danger, but she would venture deep into the huge forest all too often despite the risk of getting lost.

And that's how, one day, she discovered a treasure.

One evening, when she was running back home after her stroll in the forest, she heard a barely audible sound – a kitten's meow! But where was it? She searched for some time in vain. It was getting dark, and she was late for dinner. She failed to spot any living creatures around, so she was about to give up. Maybe it was just a bird high in the branches, she thought. Then suddenly she noticed it – there, a small furry shape was moving under the blackberry bushes! Slowly, she stretched out her hand and touched the tiny head. The kitten was so frightened that it didn't even back away, but it showed it was displeased by spitting and growling.

Ah, I would like to have seen that! Seeing such a little thing growling at Mum must have been funny! Anyway, she didn't insist.

What was this tiny kitten doing there, huddled in bushes in the middle of nowhere? It seemed so scared, crying for its mum. Where was the mother? Would she be coming to fetch her baby? Mum knew that a wild cat lived in this part of the forest; she had seen her jumping from branch to branch on several occasions.

Was the kitten lost? Had something happened to its mother? Or had she hidden it there and gone to look for dinner? What to do? Mum was at a loss. Of course, she would have liked to take the kitty, to hold it close to her – how many times had she wished she had a cat! But all this tiny creature wanted was to be reunited with its mother. If Mum had taken it away, the kitten would never see her again.

I understand her hesitation; I, too, was separated from my maman, in my case, because of that horrible yellow monster. I know how terrible it is!

For several long minutes, Mum waited, crouched near the undergrowth without making any noise, waiting for the slightest rustle of leaves. Was the mother cat going to come and fetch her kitten?

Then, regretfully, she decided to run back home – it was getting dark. At dinner, she did not speak about the kitten. It would be a waste of time; granny did not like cats, so she wouldn't understand her concerns.

But she couldn't stop thinking about the little one: what if something had happened to the mother cat?

Was the baby still in the middle of the brambles, frightened, lost, calling, hoping for its mother to come? What if a fox or a wolf passed by? Or even an owl?

As soon as dinner was over and Granny disappeared into the kitchen, Mum told her aunt about it. Ella believed in wizards and fairies. She was convinced the gentle goblins populated the forest, so she would surely know the right thing to do.

"Fetch the big torch, and let's go save the kitty!" exclaimed Ella.

That's how Kelly, a little forest girl, came to join the family. For the first few days, she lived in Ella's room, allowing Granny and Murray to get used to her. Then she moved into Murray's basket during the day and into Mum's bed at night. Secretly, because Granny, obsessed with hunting down and destroying bacteria everywhere, would not allow it. And yet, Kelly and Mum would not spend a single night apart.

As Kelly grew up, it became clear that she was a forest girl – she had all the characteristics of a wild forest cat. Little by little, her behaviour started to change. She would spend her days away from home, exploring the surroundings, and chasing field mice and voles. She would only come home for dinner, then sneak into Mum's room through the open window and under the covers to the bottom of the bed. If Granny came to inspect the room, the cat would remain invisible.

Then something happened. I'll let Mum tell the rest of the story. I see she's impatient to start.

The following spring, when Kelly was just over a year old, something surprising happened. One day, as I was sitting on the bench enjoying the first sunshine in front of the house, I saw Kelly running toward me as fast as possible. What was happening? Was she trying to escape from someone? She jumped onto my lap and rolled into a ball, purring loudly. It was unusual behaviour for her, as she was not a lap cat. Amazed, I started to cuddle her while she was still trying to settle down to find the most comfortable position. Then, suddenly, I felt something wet and warm in my lap, something moving.

I got scared, not knowing what was going on. I screamed loudly and even wanted to push the poor kitty away. By chance, I didn't. To this day, I'm sorry for having screamed! But, Freddy, how could I have known that she had just given birth to two little kittens?

Hearing my scream, Ella came running out of the house. We laughed and marvelled, and soon, we set up a comfortable basket for the little family in a quiet room in the house. Ella brought a soft blanket and something good for Kelly to eat.

My auntie found it strange that a wild forest cat couldn't find any safe place to give birth to her kittens except my lap, but I think she had the utmost faith in me. It made me happy –it confirmed that we were forever bound by love.

Kelly had given birth to two little kittens, two tabby boys like herself. She stayed in her basket with the kittens for a few days, never leaving them for more than a few minutes. She was an affectionate and super-protective mother. The two kittens were lively, constantly crawling and wiggling around within the confines of the small basket. Sometimes they even managed to climb over the side and fall, eager as they were to explore. But their mother always caught them and quickly put them back in the basket. Sometimes they bickered because they both wanted to suckle from the same teat at feeding time. But most of the time, they slept, curled up together, or hid in their mother's fur.

Then, one morning, I found the basket empty - the mother and her babies had disappeared during the night. I looked everywhere in the house, the garden, and the little summer house where we used to take our meals on hot days. They were nowhere; they had just vanished. Ella told me that mother cats take their kittens to another place they think is safer a week or two after the birth. She said not to worry; Kelly would undoubtedly return if only to claim her dinner as she always did. But I still worried about the babies. They were too small to follow her.

She didn't come back right away. I had to wait more than a week before seeing her again.

Cat-sitter

One afternoon, when I had almost given up hope, I suddenly saw Kelly coming from the forest. She was still a long way off, but I could already see her walking with difficulty. She moved forward slowly, with her front legs slightly apart, swaying from left to right to keep her balance. She would stop often, put something on the ground and wait a few minutes to catch her breath. Then she would pick up her load again and continue her way. When she got closer, I could finally see: she was bringing her babies home! She walked straight toward me. When she reached the bench on which I was sitting, she stood up on her back legs and carefully placed her load on my lap, one baby after another. She looked at me with beautiful green eyes, purred, meowed twice, then turned around and ran away, jumping happily over high grass and bushes.

You know what, Freddy? Many years have passed, and so many things have happened, but I can still see this beautiful mother cat bringing her kittens to me. It was an early afternoon on a sunny, bright day and a blackbird unfolded its beautiful melody on the opposite tree . . .a moment in life so wonderful that I wish I could relive it.

So Kelly had decided I was the cat-sitter. Again, she showed me how much she loved me by entrusting me with her most precious treasure. I was so happy to see the babies again! They were adorable and seemed quite excited to be with me. We played for a while, shared a snack of cheese and ham, and then the babies fell asleep in my arms.

After an hour or more, Kelly returned. Again, she was carrying a load, but it was much lighter this time: a dead mouse, which she laid at my feet. She meowed with a guttural sound, saying, 'here, it's for you, eat it!' She kept pushing the poor dead mouse towards me. Then, seeing that I did not want it, she climbed onto my lap and took her babies away. She gently grabbed one of them with her jaw, then the other, and using her paw, secured her grip to make sure she did not lose them on the way. She slowly left in the direction she had come from, walking a bit like a duck. It was funny and touching simultaneously, and I hoped she would often bring the babies back to me.

I didn't have to wait long. The very next day, and every day for about ten days, at about the same time, I saw her arriving towards me down the lane, carrying the little ones. She always put them on my lap with a friendly but firm meow. She seemed to say "Take care of them" in a commanding tone and then run off to her freedom. Every time she came back, she had a present for me: a dragonfly, a mouse and once even a little bird that I was quick to free because it was alive and well.

Then one day, while I was waiting for her, I saw her walking alone towards the house. Had she lost the babies? Had something happened to them? For a moment, I got afraid. As she got closer, I noticed that she frequently stopped, turned around and meowed. She was calling for someone. Soon I saw the babies appearing and disappearing between the bushes, following their mother. It was a game to them!

Would they all stay at home now that the babies were independent? I hoped so. But it wasn't to be. Kelly would bring them in for dinner in the evening, and then they would both go off with her, frolicking happily, jumping over the tall grass and bushes. Now that she had her babies, she no longer came to sleep in my bed. She was becoming increasingly independent. The house was now just a canteen for her and the kittens.

The Separation

It seemed to me that summer came faster that year, probably because of the kittens. The long school holidays were approaching. I was already looking forward to having more time for my cats and playing with them.

But my mother had other plans: she had booked me on a scout camp for the whole holiday! I was desperate. Being away from my little family for such a long time would break my heart. They were everything to me; they were my world. What would become of them without me? Kelly was incredibly attached to me – she would only accept her dinner if I stood next.

Aunt Ella promised to take care of them, and I knew I could trust her. How could you not trust a woman who believes in elves?

The day we left for camp, we ran very late, and my mum didn't allow me to search for Kelly to say good-bye. She was to drive me to the city, from where a bus would take us, scouts, to the seaside. I had never seen the sea before. We used to spend our vacations climbing the Alps. I should have been excited about the trip, but I wasn't. Thoughts of my kitty and her kids filled my mind.

How would they react when they found I was not home? I could only think of them all the way down to the seaside, and my eyes were full of tears. It didn't help that my mum and aunt had assured me the cats would be waiting for me upon my return.

Anyway, they didn't.

It was the end of August when I finally returned home. The school was due to restart soon. Of course, as soon as I arrived, I started to look for Kelly and the kittens. First in the garden, then on the outskirts of the forest and finally in the house. They were nowhere.

I looked and searched and called. I even wandered deep into the forest – in vain. At dinner, my aunt told me what had happened.

The cat had come regularly with her kittens to eat during the first week, and each time she seemed to be looking for me, meowing around the house, trying to get into my room. Then she started to show up less and less frequently. Finally, she disappeared completely. My aunt called the little family every evening and went to the forest, trying to find them, to bring them food. But she never saw Kelly again; the cat did not answer her calls. Once, she saw the two little ones at a distance, but when she called, they ran away.

"Kelly had regained her freedom as a forest cat and had taken her kids with her", said my Mum. "You can never tame a wild cat", she said. "They accept to live with people while they are young, and then one day, they go back to the forest, forever wild, forever free."

I wasn't sure I should believe this. I looked at my aunt, and she gave me a sign by winking. I knew then that this could in no way apply to Kelly.

I kept looking for her, day after day. Every time I came home from school, I expected to see her sitting on the veranda in the sun with her two little ones, all three waiting for me. As soon as I approached the house, I would start to run, full of hope. But she was never there.

Whenever I had free time, I didn't hesitate to venture deep into the forest, sometimes almost getting lost – but all my searches were in vain. Sometimes a rustle of leaves in the thickets or at the top of a tree would make me think it was Kelly, that she was somewhere near, looking at me, watching me. But I never saw her. She'd probably moved far away, to some distant part of that vast forest.

Before I knew it, winter was approaching. I hoped the little family would start feeling cold and hungry and return home.

But my Mum had more bad news for me: we would be moving! She had found a big house in the village with a beautiful garden. It was close to my school and the city where she worked.

Freddy, I felt like the earth had opened before me. What a disaster! All my chances of ever seeing Kelly again vanished in an instant.

The most foolish ideas crossed my mind. What if I refused to leave? What if I hid in the forest and stayed there, near my cat – she had to be somewhere; she couldn't have just vanished.

On the day of our departure, when everything was ready and the truck loaded with our moving boxes had already left, we put our last belongings into my mother's car – some small luggage, Murray's basket, and toys. I also took Kelly's basket – the one she had used when nursing her babies.

My mother started the car, and we slowly began to leave. Suddenly, I saw something moving on the path from the forest: a shape – no, two, three figures, approaching fast, running towards us!

"Kelly!" I shouted and jumped out of the car. "My Kelly!"

I ran towards her, and she rushed into my arms as if we had never been apart. I hugged her tightly, afraid she would change her mind and run away again, but this wasn't her plan. As I settled her next to Murray in the basket, I looked to see where the little ones were, but Aunt Ella had already grabbed them and held them in her lap.

Freddy, believe it or not, deep down in my heart, I always knew we would be reunited, Kelly and I. It just couldn't be otherwise.

* * *

Here ends Mum's story, dear reader. Back then, smartphones hadn't yet been invented, and humans didn't take pictures as often as they do today. So even though I don't have many pictures to show you, I know that they all lived happily together for many years in that village house: Kelly and her kids, Murray and the humans.

Two Guest Stories

IN WHICH FREDDY'S FRIENDS, MAGGIE (ANDY SHEPHEARD) AND MUNCH'S MUM (HELEN NICHOLSON) TELL TWO TOUCHING STORIES

Sweet Maggie is Left Behind

Told by Maggie herself, with the help of her Mum, Andy Shepheard

I was born in the summertime, but I don't remember my cat Mummy.

The earliest memories I do have are of my first home. I lived there until I was about six or seven months old. I had humans who fed me and played with me, but I spent a lot of time outside. I would go out after breakfast to explore and do important cat stuff. I always went home at night to sleep. It was a pretty good life – I had lots of cat friends and we played a lot! Then in January 2020, things started to change. I noticed a lot of boxes appearing in my home. They weren't for me to play in, though, they got filled pretty quickly. I didn't know what was going on, but as I spent a lot of time outside playing with my friends, I wasn't too bothered. I thought it was some silly human stuff going on.

However, one day, when I arrived home for tea, I found my cat flap was locked shut and when I jumped onto the window sill, the room was empty! What were the humans doing? It was all very odd. I waited and waited, but nobody appeared. It was freezing and I was starving. As the night got darker, I felt terrified. The next day, I found my cat friends and told them. One said they had seen my humans loading all the boxes into a van and driving off. I didn't know what to think. I went back to the house, but nobody appeared and I couldn't find anything to eat. I tried to keep warm by sleeping in an old dog house in the garden and spent my day foraging for scraps to eat. I was very, very scared. I didn't have the energy to play with my cat friends anymore. Days passed and I started to get even more frightened. Although I was very hungry and hadn't eaten properly for a long time, my tummy felt funny and grew bigger.

Then, one morning as I was sitting outside my house, one of the human neighbours approached me. She was a lovely lady who had often stopped to pat me before. "Oh dear, didn't they take you with them?" she asked. I meowed that I was scared in reply, but she didn't seem to understand and went into her house. I was very sad, but she came out again a few minutes later with some chicken. I was so happy to eat something that hadn't come out of a bin I gave her big head boops and tucked in greedily. "Oh dear," she said, "you poor thing!" I was sorry when she went back into her house a few minutes later. I waited, but she didn't come back that day. The next day though, she did bring me some more food and every day after that for a while. I don't know how many days, as I was still very cold and lonely. It seemed like a long while. Then one day, when she brought me food, another lady was with her. As I was eating, I heard the new lady say "yes she does look pregnant". Was this me they were talking about? Was that why my tummy was getting bigger and feeling odd? What would I do with babies? I was still a baby myself; I couldn't look after kittens!

While I was thinking all of this, the new lady had gone to her car and fetched a carrier. I had been scooped up and put on a warm blanket in the box the next thing I knew. I thought maybe she knew where my family was and would take me to them. When we arrived, my family was nowhere to be seen, but they showed me into a warm room with soft blankets and full bowls of food and clean water!

I didn't know what was happening, but I was very grateful. The lady told me that she would take care of me and help me when my babies were born. I slept well that night. A couple of weeks later, I had my babies – three little boys. Two panthers and a tabby like me. It was tough work – they were so tiny and I was exhausted. The lady was kind; she gave me fusses and helped me with my babies. The boys grew into boisterous kittens – which was even more hard work, but the lady sometimes took them for an hour and let me sleep. It seemed like a long time since I had had the energy to play. When the boys were eight weeks old, the lady explained that she had found them all loving homes to go to. She reassured me that their new families had promised never to abandon them and love them forever. I was so very sad to see them go, but it was a relief to know they would be safe and looked after.

I asked her if I had to go back to the streets now, but she said NO! I was to have an operation to make sure I didn't have more babies, but after that, I went to another foster home to recover. Then they would look for a new family of my own! The new family would also be made to promise never to abandon me and to look after me forever.

This was how I found Andy. After my operation, I went to her home to recuperate. She told me that she had had a beautiful lady cat called Scribbles who had gone over the Rainbow Bridge a few weeks before.

I was given a purple Mousie to play with that had been Scribbles and it smelt delicious. I explored the house and discovered Andy had been well trained in fusses. I was so relieved and happy to be able to play again without worrying about babies or where to find my next meal. I purred a lot. The next day, Andy asked me if I would like to stay with her forever. She said she would love me and look after me. She explained she would never abandon me and promised I would never be cold or hungry again. I knew she missed Scribbles, so I agreed. I promised to keep her company and to cuddle and play a lot! We have both kept our promises and will continue to for as long as we live. That is my story.

MAGGIE

Munch Goes Missing
Told by Munch's Mum, Helen Nicholson

T he black cat with the white heart arrived into our lives on July 2nd 2015.

It was a hot summer's day, and he walked in through the open patio doors. He lay down on the mat and was super friendly, even requesting some belly rubs. Richard offered him some ham from the fridge, which he gobbled up enthusiastically. He was a happy boy, purring and making biscuits on the bean bag we had put on the mat.

From that moment, we think he decided this could be his new home. He spent the next few weeks coming and going as he pleased and sitting on my lap when I came home from work. He would leave at night to go off on his patrols.

Then it was time for us to go off on one of our holidays to Greece. I set up a shelter outside in the garden for him. We decided that if he was still waiting for us when we got back, he must surely want to adopt us.

Sure enough, within a few hours of returning from holiday, he was back, asking to come inside. We decided to look for missing cat posters around the estate, check out local social media groups, and take him to the vet to see if he was chipped. They confirmed he wasn't chipped and estimated his age to be two based on his teeth. The vet asked if we wanted to chip him and register him to us, so we did! And that was that; we decided to call him Munchkin, on Grandpa's suggestion, and his adoption of us as his humans was complete.

Later on, Munchkin became affectionately known as Munch Pudding based on a family tradition of everyone being called Pud. Munch, for short.

From 2015 to 2019, we spent four and a half happy years together, including a few trips to the vets for minor injuries. Munch loved to be outside, it was what made him happy, exploring his territory and keeping everything in order.

Then, one Sunday night, December 8th, 2019, Munch did not come home. At the time, he was much more nocturnal than now, so whilst I was worried, this wasn't totally out of character, and I hoped he was just having an adventure and would come home in the morning. But as I went off to work, Munch still hadn't returned. I thought this was odd. I drove home at lunch time, but he hadn't returned. When I returned from work later that evening, my heart sank when I realised he wasn't there waiting for me.

After a couple of days, the friends I had made on #CatsOfTwitter started to ask why I hadn't posted pictures of Munch for a while, so we told Phoebe and Juno what had happened. They immediately helped to spread the word, as did many others. Everyone was so kind and supportive and gave me lots of advice about what to do.

I searched for Munch every day in the evenings and early mornings and grew increasingly worried. I missed him so much. Then the weather turned dreadful. I will never forget the torrential rain as I searched for him desperately, unable to bear thinking of him being out in that weather for so long.

We ordered posters, and I walked around our estate with a little step ladder, tying the picture of his beautiful face to as many lampposts as I could. I also dropped posters into the local shops and pubs. People on #CatsOfTwitter encouraged me to leaflet all the houses near me, so I ordered 4,000. Richard and I leafleted 1,000s of homes until our hands were sore from pushing them through all the letterboxes.

Whilst I had moments of despair, because of the support from people of on #CatsOfTwitter, I never gave up hope that Munch would find his way home. We had several reported sightings, raising my hopes, but each turned out not to be Munch.

My world stopped turning in those ten days. I just felt completely empty. The house seemed devoid of life without him, and all his beds, food, and toys were a constant reminder he was missing. Christmas was on hold.

Then on December 18th, at around 11.30 pm, a lady called and said she thought she could hear meowing coming from her garage. My heart skipped a few beats. Amazingly, she was only two streets away. I had walked past that house many times, calling out for my boy. I asked if I could go to her home straight away. I ran there, and she answered the door, tossing the garage keys over to me. My hands shaking, I started to unlock her garage and I could hear the same meows. As the door opened, Munch ran into my arms, and I lifted him, totally overcome with emotion. He felt as light as a feather. So, light that I had to check for a moment, it was definitely him! And there it was his white heart.

I thanked the lady profusely and then carried Munch home in my arms, talking to him all the way. He was looking all around him, wide-eyed, taking in the sights and smells of the streets that were familiar to him. He was wriggling by the time we got to the front door, but I wasn't about to let him go. I opened the front door and he ran into his home, sniffing everything!

He wanted to eat right away and enjoyed a hearty meal, but he was careful not to overeat. Then he wanted to drink, he was so thirsty. So, I sat with him whilst he lapped up the water from the dripping bath tap. The feeling of relief and pure happiness was immense. I slept holding him on the bed all night, and I kept waking up to check he was still there.

My precious boy was back home and it was a Christmas miracle. The best Christmas ever.

MUNCH

We Say Goodbye

Yesterday morning, Mum woke me up with joyful cries: "Freddy, Freddy! Get up! Your book came out this morning! Soon you'll be famous, my boy!"

I jumped to the window excitedly. I'd been waiting for this day for so long!

But oh, what a disappointment! I looked everywhere and couldn't spot a single copy of my book in the garden! Why wasn't it there? Mum said it had "come out". When my friends come out from behind the hedges, I can see them. Of course, I expected the same would happen with my book: a thousand copies should be covering my garden – they should be hanging from the rosebushes, swinging happily on the branches of the trees, marching on the lawn, calling out to me: "Freddy, Freddy, here we are! Come, turn our pages! Look inside! Aren't we beautiful?"

But there was not a single copy of my book in the garden. I heard no hoorays, no bravos. All would have been silent were it not for the mocking song of our two blackbirds. And the worst was that no one was queuing outside our garden gate! If the book had come out, surely endless queues of fans would be waiting in front of our house. Aren't always queues when a new mobile phone is released?

Something was not quite right.

There was only one possible explanation: Mum must have got the day wrong!

"Mum, are you sure my book is out?" I asked a little doubtfully.

"Of course, sweety, look it up on Amazon!"

Amazon? Where could that be? Some neighbouring garden I don't know? I pulled the world map from Mum's bookshelf. And I searched and searched.

Well, it took time to find it. And you know what? It was a river! "The greatest river in the world", said the map. How could anyone publish a book on a river, I wondered. Maybe there was a garden somewhere around? Yes, there was, and a very huge one at that. A rainforest, it's called. Oh, wow! There must be plenty of cats, I thought and searched further. But I could only find some big cats named "jaguars". They looked fierce; very unlikely buyers, I believe! And the worst was to come: the river was full of caimans and piranhas! You can easily imagine what would happen to my book in such a place. The few copies that would not instantly sink to the bottom of the giant Amazon would be devoured by crocodiles or torn to pieces by furious piranhas...

Oh, poor me. I had invested so much love in this book. Now, my hard work will be wasted, forever buried in the depths of that gigantic Amazon. . .

I had to have a word with Mum immediately. Luckily for her, she had already gone to the market. Pffft!

Depressed and sad, I decided to go to the park and never return home. But no sooner had I taken a few steps into the garden than I saw my friends coming towards me. They were marching steadily and had such angry faces that I became frightened.

"Hello, pals," I said, smiling nervously. "What brings you here? Come in; Mum has bought lots of treats!"

Sometimes a few treats can make the day a little sweeter.

While they were following me to the terrace, I thought of all the excuses I could – I knew they had come to complain about my book. I figured I should say something like the printer is out of ink; the keyboard keys have become tangled; the word processor has gone haywire; Mum has served a meal that's too hot, and there aren't any sunny spots in the living room. . . . All the little things that depress a writer in no time and dry up their imagination forever.

You see, I knew exactly what they were going to say. There were stories I had written but hadn't published; others that had been told to me but I hadn't yet written; still more in which my imagination had sometimes strayed a little too far and so on.

I invited my friends to sit around the garden table, which became a conference table for the occasion. And indeed, no sooner had we sat down than they started to talk and talk. The reproaches accumulated from minute to minute, and my friends looked more and more threatening.

What was the best strategy? Should I start running away to escape?

Then it dawned on me. I stood up and shouted: "The book has been published on Amazon!"

And you know what? All the reproaches stopped dead in their tracks. Complete silence reigned in the garden for a few seconds, so great was the deception. They knew it at once. Their beautiful stories would be buried inside the depths of the Amazon, together with three hundred million other self-published books, with little or no chance of ever surfacing again.

A murmur of despair followed.

"Ah?" said some.

"What a pity!" sighed others.

And Big Head added with a touch of sadness:

"Is that true, Freddy? Will no one ever know that I, Big Head, invented the magic garden?"

The fox from the lake replied: "Dummy, it was me, not you!" They looked at each other in a fury, and I feared they would start fighting.

Luckily, Mum came along and shouted: "Freddy, already three copies of your book have sold! Can you imagine! The sales have started!"

"Three copies?" marvelled my friends. "Hurray! Viva, Freddy! You hit it! It's a beast-seller!"

"Bestseller," corrected Mum.

"Have they read my story?" asked the anxious Big Head. "Have they learnt how I invented. . . ." But he caught the flames from the fox and opted not to continue.

Daddy Cat Uddy enquired if there were any copies left. "Because you know, I want to send some to Pegasus and Benedict!"

As for myself, I was starting to feel happy. And grateful. So I climbed on a chair and shouted as loud as I could (you know, some of my readers live far away): "Thank you, dear readers, whether you are one or a hundred or a thousand! Thank you for joining us in the magic garden!"

"Yes, thank you," shouted my friends with me. "We love you!"

Mum ran back to the kitchen to organise the "book launch party", as she put it. What was this? Incredible, my mum! First, she goes and publishes my stories on the largest river ever, and then she wants us to "launch" the book! Where to? Just so, in the air?

We didn't have any copies, and besides, how would that be useful?

However, the word "party" manifested magic. Suddenly, the garden was bustling with activity: Big Head and the fox placed more chairs around the table, Cannelle started picking flowers for decoration, and Thad jumped into the jar of water (although I think this may have been unintentional). Chili asked how to light the barbecue, but Daddy Cat Uddy said it was too dangerous and that we'd have to make do without it. Fifi, Joey and Lulu began to dance on the lawn, and Mummy Tahiti set about arranging the cups and saucers on the table. Everything had to be purr-fect, she said.

The cats from the neighbourhood heard something about the book "becoming a beast-seller" and rang the doorbell to join the party. Soon, there were over fifty guests in the garden. I think so because, if you remember, I can only count to twelve.

Mum soon returned from the kitchen with plates full of treats, and the party started – the best ever, in my opinion. Big Head and the fox were in charge of the music, and I can tell you that they sang totally off-key. But no one noticed because we were too happy to have sold three whole books in one day.

Please, don't tell anybody that two of them were bought by Mum.

Now, we all have to say goodbye to you, dear reader. But we will be back soon. We have many other stories to share with you.

With lots of love from Freddy's Magic Garden.

Printed in Great Britain
by Amazon

11353691R00210